The Forgotten Civilization

Steven R. Willis

Printed in the United States of America

GoToPublish LLC
1-888-337-1724
www.gotopublish.com
info@gotopublish.com

CONTENTS

I am dedicating this book to my loving wife, Margaret Willis. We started this journey together with doing research and talking for hours about what we had found. She is unable to be here at its completion because of cancer. She went home on January 18, 2022, and is dearly missed by all the family.

FOREWORD

I've watched the TV show *Ancient Aliens* for a number of years, and I've had a problem with the program's assumption that Bible stories and other accounts from ancient civilizations that talk about Sky Beings, are all accounts of Alien encounters. Another plausible explanation for all of these events would be encounters with good and fallen Angels. Accounts from other ancient civilizations that speak of witnessing a war between the gods in flying machines using strange weapons are actually true. This is backed up by scripture and Archeology. For some reason, these scriptures have been ignored by the Christian establishment church. I believe the reason for this is that these scriptures talk about truths the church would rather not discuss.

This could be one of the reasons why the church of old rejected the Apocrypha Books back in 300 AD. They just didn't want to discuss the content of those books. Ancient stories from all over the world were also summarily dismissed in the same way. Discarded but not forgotten, these stories and books have resurfaced in the last 50 years or so. I feel that the Apocrypha Books and ancient stories offer truths and historical content that are useful in understanding what happened in our ancient past. After all, they cost someone a lot of time and effort to produce. Quite a lot of their content has been verified through archeological finds and astronomical confirmation of Celestial events documented in these stories by the NASA computing system. For this reason, I have included selective portions that I believe add some clarity to this narrative.

Humans have developed the bad habit of rejecting ancient texts simply because we don't understand a portion of them. This current generation has cultivated intolerance to the degree that we are banning and burning books if only one or a small number object to any of their contents. As many previous generations have discovered, this is not a wise mindset to cultivate. By offending a small minority of people, The Bible and Christians have now become the target, but this is not new. For many years, it has been acceptable to say the Bible is full of lies and fairytales, even though that has itself been proven wrong time and again. It seems that Christianity and Jesus have become the only acceptable things to be intolerant of. The latest AI advancement available online is ChatGPT, and on the surface, it seems like it could be very helpful. It will write you a paper on any subject, including Buddha, Mohamed, or any religion. However, if you ask it to produce a paper on Jesus, the program will decline, saying He is too controversial to be written about. Yet, if one searches with an open mind, they will find the Bible is full of truth.

These truths include the fact that God created the dinosaurs and the Earth millions of years ago, along with the constellations and the universe. Next is that Lucifer ruled the Earth thousands of years ago (for how long, it is impossible to know). Then he rebelled and tried to overthrow God. He lost that war, of course, but it was because of this that this world was destroyed in the first flood. We compare Lucifer's flood to Noah's flood a little later in this book. Also, there is a vast amount of physical evidence available to back up these ignored scriptures. And it is this Forgotten Civilization and hidden knowledge that this book attempts to expose.

For many years (centuries, actually), the Church has incorrectly claimed that the Earth is only 6,000 years old. This has caused many seekers of truth to turn away from learning the glorious truths about God. Please don't misunderstand me here. I do believe in the prophetic timelines laid out in scripture. Those being that there will be 6,000 years of time from Adam to the second return of Christ at Armageddon. The Bible speaks of five major kingdoms before His return. The major kingdoms prophesied are Babylon, Persia, Greece, and Rome. Following Rome, there would be a large period of time where God stopped dealing with the world through Israel. This occurred because Israel rejected Jesus as their Messiah, and this period of time is generally known as the Church Age, which would roughly be a period of 2000 years. This period of time is the final dispensation of Daniel's prophecy (Daniel 7:2–8). The first part ended with Jesus' death due to Israel's rejection of Him as their Messiah.

The last kingdom that is to be set up in the world is a One World Government, having a One World Religion. It will be based in a United Europe headed by a man called the Antichrist in scripture. This is already well on its way to being set up, in case you haven't been paying attention.

After he kills off almost two-thirds of the Earth's population, he will be finally destroyed at the Battle of Armageddon by Jesus himself. Following that, a period of 1,000 years called the Millennium occurs, during which Jesus reigns over the Earth from Jerusalem. He will reign over all nations (Isaiah 2:4; 42:1), and the world will have peace (Isaiah 11:6–9). Satan will be bound and gagged at the beginning of this reign (Revelation 20:1–3), and everyone will worship Jesus for that time (Isaiah 2:2–3). The Earth becomes like the Garden of Eden before Satan's last attempted rebellion (Joel 2:3).

But what this book is speaking about is a time long before Adam when Lucifer reigned here on Earth (Ezekiel 28:2–18, OKJV). A time that ended with Lucifer and the third of the angels (who followed him) rebelling to overthrow God but losing. Remember, Satan was already a fallen angel when he tempted Eve in the Garden (Genesis 3:1–7). Now Jeremiah (4:23–28 OKJV) details the results of God's judgment on Satan and the world he created before Adam. It was total and complete, where nothing survived. You'll see that Jeremiah 4:23 echoes Genesis 1:2. This book exposes Satan and his minions attempts to hide these facts and confuse the world with their false theories of Evolution, the Big Bang Theory, and UFOs.

In the following chapters, you will learn about mistranslations in scripture, hidden truths about God's creation process, and read scriptural truths about what God said truly happened. You will see evidence from fossil finds that proves men and Giants walked with and hunted dinosaurs. You will also see scriptures showing that Lucifer ruled the Earth before his rebellion and long before Adam's creation. Plus the fact that Lucifer's world was utterly destroyed after his rebellion by the first flood, and I don't mean Noah's flood (Jeremiah 4:23–28). There is scriptural evidence that shows these truths very plainly, so you can read and see the truth for yourselves from God's Word. You will learn about and understand the time gap that exists between Genesis 1:1 and Genesis 1:2. I will also demonstrate to the readers why Darwin's Theory of Evolution is and always has been impossible. My hope is that these truths will reopen the minds of true seekers who have been turned away by the false teachings of past generations.

CHAPTER ONE

This book is about a time in the distant past. Long before Adam, ancient humans and dinosaurs were ruled by an extraterrestrial race of angels. Not only were they not from this planet, but they weren't even from this dimension. You may not believe it, but it is also spoken of in the Bible. The Bible tells us where they came from and the name of their leader. Lucifer was his name. He was a high-ranking cherubim. Also, the Bible speaks of his life before he came to Earth, and who gave him the position of Covering Cherub over Earth (Ezekiel 28:14).

Lucifer was sent here to develop a civilization with the humans of that time period. Archeology tells us that at one point in our distant past, there were eight different humanoids living on Earth at the same time. All were rudimentary in their development. So Lucifer had to start from scratch. He had to train a workforce that could develop cities, nations, industries, culture, and religion. In part, he was successful, but his methods were all wrong. Lucifer took the easy way, and we'll talk about that later. The Bible tells us that when he was in heaven, he was perfect in all his ways and full of wisdom. After a period of time leading this project on Earth, he became proud and full of himself. So much so that he rebelled and talked one-third of the angels into following him in that folly. They lost, of course, and the Bible tells us that God destroyed everything Lucifer had built plus all life on Earth in the first catastrophic flood. Yes, I said the first flood, as we'll explain later in Chapter 3.

Today, we can only see fragments of Lucifer's cities and temples all around the Earth through the archeological excavations that are occurring. All ancient cultures around the world have stories of a catastrophic flood that ended an advanced civilization because the gods were angry at them. True to a point. This flood has mistakenly been taken as Noah's flood, but it wasn't. However, our Intellectual Elites around the world are actively hiding or destroying evidence that shows the truth of that time period. They are doing this because they are protecting their accepted dogma that Darwin was right and intelligent men didn't exist before 30,000 years ago, that they were only hunter-gatherers. Even this timeline has changed many times in the past due to discoveries in archeology and science that they couldn't hide. One example is Gobekli Tepe in Turkey.

They are searching for proof of Darwin's theory and finding none. The study of UFOs has become popular in the last century, but researchers are hiding what they are finding. Archeology and Science are corrupted because they are trying to find proof of their accepted dogmas and timelines. None are even looking in the Bible, where the truth can be found (as you'll see further on.) They are attacking the Bible at every turn, calling it fairytales and fiction. I've heard it many times that God is not real and Jesus was only a prophet. Well, let's address the accusation of it being lies and fairytales.

***

The Bible predicted in Daniel 12:1 that there would come **a time of trouble for the Jewish people**, greater than any they have seen since Israel first came into existence as a nation. That prophecy played out from 1938 to 1945, when Hitler killed six million of them in his purge to purify the German race.

In the Bible, it was prophesied that **Israel would become a nation again** after a long, world-wide dispersal (Matthew 24:32–34; Isaiah 11:11–12). This was thought to be an impossible occurrence, but it became a fact on May 14, 1948, after almost 2000 years of dispersal around the world.

Jesus foretold Israel retaking Jerusalem (Luke 21:22–24). He said Jerusalem would be conquered by the Gentiles until the Time of the Gentiles came to an end. Israel retook Jerusalem in the 1967 Six-Day War. President Donald Trump recognized it officially as Israel's capital on December 6, 2017.

It is interesting to note that the Bible prophesied that **in the End Times, travel would increase and knowledge would explode** (Daniel 12:4). Keep in mind that this was written around 2700 years ago, while Israel was in Babylonian captivity. We live in a time where knowledge just seems to expand exponentially every year. At the beginning of my life, there was no TV, no refrigerator, and phones were mounted on the wall. You spoke to an operator, who dialed the number for you. Milk and dairy products were delivered to your door by a milkman riding in a horse-driven cart; streetcars were still pulled by horses, etc.

Yes, I'm fairly old. Most of the modern conveniences have been developed since my birth, and I've had to adjust to each new development and invention as they came out. So when the Bible stated, "In the End Times, there will be an explosion of knowledge," I could completely relate, and now the explosion is teaching itself in the form of AI. Daniel also spoke of the increase in travel in the End Times. Well, with the advent of cars, trains, and planes, there isn't a place on Earth that you can't reach in less than a day. Remember, it took Columbus 10 weeks to cross the Atlantic, and it takes us only a few hours by plane, not including waiting for our luggage, and we complain about that.

Has anyone ever told you that **the Bible prophesied the development of television, computers, cell phones, the internet, and satellite communications?** Well, it did! In Revelation 11:3–11 NIV, it tells the story of two men who will be speaking against the dictator of that time (The Antichrist). He'll get fed up with them and have them killed. He won't allow their bodies to be buried, but he'll leave them in the streets of Jerusalem for three and a half days. The News Media will put a ring of cameras around them and constantly broadcast that image around the world in every language to every nation around the world. And when those people see their dead bodies, they will celebrate and party. That's a gruesome scene, but think about it for a moment. In 1979, the Ayatollah of Iran broadcast the dead bodies of the American Marines after the failed attempt at rescue. Same principle. But that and this further event in Jerusalem would not be possible if Satellite Communications, TV, Cell Phones, Computers, and the Internet didn't exist.

These prophecies are all indicators of the Last Generation before Jesus returns to Earth and sets up His kingdom here. There are many more, but I won't list them here. In short, the truth is that we are living in a generation where it is prophesied that Jesus will return. Are you ready? The Bible is the source of truth! It is not a fairytale.

***

Aldous Huxley once said, "Facts do not cease to exist because they are ignored."

As true a statement as you will ever see, the reason for writing this book is the fact that tomorrow is not a guarantee for anyone, and tomorrow will not come for all of us sooner or later. The fact for us all is that our time on Earth is limited, so spend it well. This is what I've learned in my time here, and as I move closer to the end and a new beginning, I feel deeply sorry for the young people who don't understand God. Because life doesn't end with death. It is a door everyone has to pass through in order to start our next phase of life. The purpose of life is not only to start a family and support them financially, but it is also to guide them and teach them how to judge the truth and make their decisions based on those truths, not other people's opinions of those truths. The foundational truth is that we must find God. Then we must learn about Him and make a decision based on that knowledge whether to believe the Bible or not.

Here's a shortcut for you: The Bible is true, and I'll prove it in this book. The Devil is real, and he's not our friend. He's doing a marvelous job of hiding this truth from the world, and it all starts with his question to each of us, just as he asked Eve, "Did God really say?" You see, if he can get you to doubt, even a little bit, that the Bible is true, he has won his objective. He is trying to plant this doubt about the Bible in each and every human in an attempt to keep us from trying to learn about God. There is no other religion in the world where the devil is trying so hard to keep people from even studying it. All of his efforts are focused on causing people to doubt that the Bible is even remotely true. And he has been quite successful in this effort to cause people to believe the Bible is nothing but fairytales.

However, like everything else we learn in life, we should determine the truth of the Bible for ourselves. This book was written to help you say, "I see you, devil, you black-hearted SOAB, and I will not be fooled anymore!" This book will show you the truth that has been hidden from the general public for centuries. You will see the pictorial evidence, along with scriptures from the Bible, coupled with archaeological and scientific evidence that proves there was an ancient and very advanced civilization here on Earth, long before Adam and the Genesis story.

***

I am shocked by what I've seen and by what God has led me to in the Bible. By this, I know the Bible is real and full of truth, history, and prophecy. His word shows us the true story He is telling. I have seen how the Bible, archeology, science, and ancient stories confirm each other. And knowing and understanding the Biblical truths, we will not be easily fooled by the lies and schemes of the devil. Through God's wisdom, we can see the evidence in archaeology, which was carved in stone so many millennia ago. With open hearts and minds, we can see the truth found in the pages of scripture. Truths that are echoed and embellished upon in the ancient stone tablets and temple walls from ages long past. This is the truth that the Intellectual Elites of the world have us willfully ignore because those truths don't fit their accepted dogmas and timelines. Ancient truths that have been willfully ignored by these men and women who support Satan's agenda to keep hidden the evidence from the past that shows the Bible is true. The Intellectual Elites of our societies around the world have, for over a century, controlled what the public is told about and shown about the discoveries in Archeology and Science. They control what is written in our children's textbooks and what is displayed in our Museums. As you'll see, they ignore and have hidden a vast amount of evidence that has been unearthed. However, ignoring these facts does not make them any less true.

God shows us in His word that Lucifer ruled here on Earth before Adam. He is not afraid of telling the truth. We can start to determine this because the Bible also tells us the devil was already a fallen angel when he tempted Eve. Thus the described events of Lucifer's rule happened before Adam and Eve. The prophet Jeremiah tells us of a man-made civilization that Lucifer reigned over and that it was destroyed by God before Adam. You'll see this has been confirmed by archeological discoveries that have been misdated and misinterpreted. Therefore the Creationist timeline of only 6,000 years for Earth's existence doesn't work. Age and dispensation are two different things.

God's creation story has had many stages and it has been much longer than we've been led to believe. The fact that Lucifer's civilization existed long before Adam also puts the Intellectual Elites estimate that man has only existed for 30,000 years out the window. According to the Bible and archeological discoveries men existed in an advanced civilization for hundreds of thousands of years before Adam. That is the theory that this book is testing. **Did man exist in an advanced civilization before Adam?**

According to Marvin L. Lubenow's book "Bones of Contention", we have two things at work here: Faith and Science. Now he has researched the fossil issue for over 25 years so he has experience to draw from. He says that Science should be a self-correcting faith. The Scientists postulate on an idea and then proceed to find evidence to prove or disprove the original assumption. For example, Edison found 999 ways not to make a light bulb and on the 1000th try he succeeded. Bell had a similar experience with the telephone. They both self-corrected their original theories until they found the right combination or in other words the truth. Some scientists just like the search. Finding fulfillment in determining what supports their theories and what doesn't. They should have kept track of what supported their original theory and what didn't. And if they found the original theory was unsupported, throw it out and start a new theory supported by their recent discoveries.

In this way, Science should be a self-correcting mechanism, but it isn't. It has been discovered that personal belief, current dogma, secure research funding and acceptance by peer groups all have a huge impact on scientific research. Scientists who are evolutionists have a very tenuous relationship with the truth. This becomes very apparent in their rush to find the elusive missing link to man and animals. Since Darwin's publication in 1859, there have been many frauds put forward as proof of this missing link.

- Java man in the 1890s,
- Ramapithecus Man in 1904,
- Piltdown Man in 1912,
- Nebraska Man in 1920,
- Lucie in the 1930s

All of which have been proven to be fakes for the missing link. Yet we still see them in full color renderings in school textbooks and displayed in museums around the world as facts that men evolved from apes. There have also been numerous fakes put forward for the missing links of evolution in the animal kingdom, all eventually proved to be fake, but no retractions have ever been given. Now all research on the original bones is being strictly regulated. If the researcher is known not to agree with the dogma of the person in charge of the bones they will not be given access for research or funding. Today, it is plainly visible that the Intellectual Elites of the world are deeply entrenched in evolution and vehemently oppose any proof to the contrary.

So this means that it is up to Christians to look and see if there is any corroborating evidence for Lucifer's reign? As it turns out, there is. Lucifer's time period was documented to some extent on Sumerian stone tablets and in ancient writings and carved into the walls of ancient temples by that long deceased civilization. These truths scream to us from the ancient stone. The scriptures themselves tell us that a world with cities and nations which were inhabited by humans was here long ago. When we examine scripture + Paleontology + Zoology + Archeology + ancient stories, we find they add up to a Lost Civilization. Because few have taken the evidence from all these areas of study this truth has been hidden from us all for centuries. Some people have noticed how some of these facts are incompatible with the world's accepted dogma. But, no one has put them all together or associated them with the fact of Lucifer's ancient civilization which is recorded in the Bible. The reality of Lucifer's civilization existing on Earth many millennium before Adam answers so many questions.

You see, the Bible plainly teaches us that God has the infinite power and ability to create and control this entire Universe. Common sense shouts to us that it took some time to accomplish this, judging from the detailed work that was done by hand in the Genesis story. The world's Intellectual Elite specialists, and I use the word *specialist* liberally, are really big on forming theories. The theory of The Big Bang, Evolution, and theories of how long men have been on Earth and when men came out of caves, etc. However, they have run headlong into trouble with these theories. During the last 40 years new technology and advancements in science have shown them to be dead wrong, but these discussions are taboo.

Even though the *Ancient Aliens* TV program's quote the Bible frequently, they always classify the verses as UFO encounters. They obviously know very little about the Bible and even less about God. The Bible tells us that God is an eternal spirit being and that He lives in a different dimension, which is closely associated with ours. This is demonstrated many times in scripture, and again this information has been ignored. In the Bible, we are also told that one of God's days is equal to one-thousands of our years. Common sense tells us that the spirit beings He calls angels are governed for their lifespan by God's dimensional timeline. In other words, they don't age at the same pace we humans do. It's like comparing our lifespan to that of an ant. In scriptures we are told of the many encounters that humans have had with the angels and God's very advanced technology. This information has also been ignored or misinterpreted.

Today, we have UFO encounters or sightings as well, but there is a difference that we have to keep in mind when distinguishing these encounters. We must remember that Satan has the same technology as God. He has this technology because he was given free access to God's technology for him to accomplish the task of Covering Cherub which God appointed him as (Ezekiel 28:14). Satan did not return all this technology after he was defeated in his attempted coup of God. Also, he has more than likely repaired some of these vehicles that were damaged in that war. We can't forget he is an enemy of God and has already seen enormous and devastating defeat at the hands of God long before Adam and Eve. This forgotten civilization with its nations and cities that Lucifer had created on Earth were all destroyed after he was defeated. He hates everything about God and therefore everything God loves and that would include humans. Therefore, Satan hates us and he is actively working against us to take as many humans to Hell with him as he can.

In light of this new information we can deduce that every hostile UFO encounter (e.g. kidnappings, animal mutilations, etc.) would involve the fallen angels. Satan has worked diligently through every method and temptation he can think of to bring us down. He has done that very successfully since he took rulership of the Earth back from Adam. We effectively live in a war zone whether we know it or not. If humans choose to ignore that fact and keep buying into his lie that he doesn't exist, we do it at our own peril.

In these last days, God is ready to expose the truth. It's time to turn the lights on and let these facts speak for themselves. Satan and his co-conspirators have worked diligently over thousands of years to cause humans to believe the Bible is not true, but just a collection of fairytales. In this endeavor, he has been very successful. He has offered up competing theories like the Theory of Evolution and the Big Bang Theory. Also, through the Intellectual Elites and entities they control, Satan has been destroying, hiding or limiting access for further study and exploration on new sites. By subtly doing this, he is effectively making the evidence that would prove the Bible to be accurate to be non-existent for all intents and purposes.

Satan's biggest success in recent years is placing people who are faithful to him in positions of power in Governments all over the world. Many national leaders such as Canadian Prime Minister Justin Trudeau and 8 of his cabinet ministers are graduates of the World Economic Forum. The WEF brags about its graduates leading countries, businesses and financial institutions around the world. These graduates all have a "One World Government" agenda. This is a hidden agenda that they try never to bring up when they are campaigning for office. However, once in office, their decisions are plainly leading in that direction. With them also as heads of business, finance and tech companies, he has manipulated the Media which is one of his greatest successes. Now, if something even remotely proves a truth in the Bible, his people in the Media simply ignore it.

Remember that old joke, "If a tree falls in the forest and no one's around to hear it, does it make a sound?" Now, when events or discoveries are not reported to the people, you and me, ask the obvious, "Has it really happened?" The true answer is yes, but usually we do not know about it. Then, the result is even though it is a fact, the lack of widespread coverage in the Media means no one hears about it. So, for all intents and purposes, it effectively does not exist. Here in this book, I'm going to show you some of those facts that have been conveniently ignored, and you can decide for yourselves what is true or not.

CHAPTER 2

The Forgotten Civilization of Lucifer

In this chapter, the argument for truth begins by exposing the false teachings against it. Then we will examine scriptures that have been altered through mistranslation (possibly on purpose) or completely ignored. Keep an open mind and let the facts and common sense speak for themselves. You will also see, perhaps for the first time, the scriptures that tell of an advanced civilization prior to Adam and Eve that was ruled by Lucifer and his angels before he rebelled.

What you will learn here in no way takes away from the Biblical Story. On the contrary, the truths you'll read about in here expand on the Biblical Story and give you more insight into God, Jesus, The Holy Spirit and the Devil. This was a turbulent time in Earth's vast history that has been willfully ignored by both sides of the debate. Creationists hold to 6,000 years as the total time man, animals and the Earth have existed, and Evolutionists hold to an indefinite time period. As you'll see, it is plainly written about in scripture and has been there from the beginning. It is a fact that the Bible does not teach that this Earth began only 6,000 years ago.

The Bible tells us in Genesis that God created the Earth, constellations and the Universe. Isaiah 45:18 tells us that when He created the Earth it was perfect and ready for habitation and not empty. This is where the Gap Theory comes into play. It speaks of a time gap between verses one and two of Genesis chapter one. Because Genesis 1:2 describes the Earth as being without form and void, totally covered in water and in complete darkness. It sounds a bit confusing, but keep in mind that we don't have all the information pertaining to this topic just yet.

You see, studying the Bible is a bit like putting a puzzle together. You have to find all the scriptures that are throughout the Bible which speak on the subject you are studying. Then you will get the entire thought that God was communicating.

For example, if you wanted to know what the sign on Jesus' cross said and who wrote it, you would have to gather that information from all four gospels.

> Matthew 27:37 And set up over his head his accusation written, This Is Jesus The King Of The Jews.
>
> Mark 15:26 And the superscription of his accusation was written over, The King Of The Jews.
>
> Luke 23:38 And a superscription also was written over him in letters of Greek, and Latin, and Hebrew, This Is The King Of The Jews.
>
> John 19:19-22 **19** And Pilate wrote a title, and put it on the cross. And the writing was Jesus Of Nazareth The King Of The Jews. **20** This title then read many of the Jews: for the place where Jesus was crucified was nigh to the city: and it was written in Hebrew, and Greek, and Latin. **21** Then said the chief priests of the Jews to Pilate, Write not, The King of the Jews; but that he said, I am King of the Jews. **22** Pilate answered, What I have written I have written.

What the Sign on the Cross Says: Pilate wrote the sign, and put it on the cross. He set this accusation up over Jesus' head. It was written in Hebrew, and Greek, and Latin, and the writing was This Is Jesus Of Nazareth, The King Of The Jews. This sign was then read by many of the Jews who passed by the execution site at Golgotha. For the place where Jesus was crucified was nigh to the city of Jerusalem.

Notice that the Priests objected: Then said the chief priests of the Jews to Pilate, "Write not, The King of the Jews; but that he said, I am King of the Jews." Pilate answered, "What I have written I have written."

Do you see now? To get the complete information about the sign, you had to go to four different books of the Bible. This is true for any subject you wish to study in the Bible. It takes time and diligent effort.

The problem is that most people don't want to, or feel that they can't dedicate that kind of time to studying the scriptures. However, God told us through His communication in Joshua 1:8 that He wants us to do just that and meditate and talk about it all the time. But most of us know life gets in the way of that and we rely on Sunday sermons, memory cards in a box on the table or we'll buy a book on a particular subject we are interested in. The problem with this is that the thoughts and teachings of God are not getting deeply into your hearts or minds. You also take the chance that the author, preacher or teacher has a particular point of view or dogma that doesn't match up with the scriptures completely. And because you don't have a good grasp on the scriptures yourself, you'll miss the uneasy feeling that's trying to tell you what you're hearing or reading is not correct.

You've already seen (in The Sign on the Cross) that there are many different books of the Bible involved for each subject you may be studying in scripture. Would it surprise you to know that there are actually several books of the Bible that have information pertaining to Lucifer reigning here on Earth before Adam? You'll see as we progress forward in this book that an advanced civilization did exist here on Earth in the distant past, and the time period where it existed falls smack dab between Genesis 1:1 and Genesis 1:2. The proof for this will come from scripture, archeology and science. Now let's get started through the scriptures pertaining to this topic.

> 2 Peter 3:1-7
>
> **1** This second epistle, beloved, I now write unto you; in both which I stir up your pure minds by way of remembrance: **2** That ye may be mindful of the words which were spoken before by the holy prophets, and of the commandment of us the apostles of the Lord and Savior: **3** Knowing this first, that there shall come in the last days scoffers, walking after their own lusts, **4** And saying, Where is the promise of his coming? For since the fathers fell asleep, all things continue as they were from the beginning of the creation.

Here we see a little bit of prophecy about the last days and the people's attitude in that time toward the Bible. This generation that we live in likes to mock the Bible and Jesus's followers at every opportunity. They call believers gullible and naive fools, which we are not by any stretch of the imagination.

> 1 Peter 3:**5** For this they **willfully forget**: that by the word of God the heavens were of old, and the Earth standing out of water and in the water, **6** by which **the world *that* then existed perished, being flooded with water.**

Here we see the missing puzzle piece exposed. Since the scholars today are willingly ignoring the scriptures about Lucifer's reign they relate the first flood that God is speaking about here as Noah's flood and that is where their error begins. This first flood took place many thousands of years before Adam was created.

> 1 Peter 3:**7** But the heavens and the Earth *which* are now preserved by the same word, are reserved for fire until the day of judgment and perdition of ungodly men.

Well, we know from fulfilled prophecy that this is speaking of the Last Days. However, we need to look at more scriptures to fully understand how we got here. So let's look at the scriptures which speak of the beginning of creation. The Bible gives us insights about God's creation process, not in total detail and specifics, but meaningful insights into what He did or might have done. It tells us God and the angels are from another dimension, and He created this dimension and began speaking the substance of faith into this dimension. Science tells us that there was an initial starting point, but they call it their Big Bang Theory (everything created through accidental collision of random space rocks). However, the Bible tells us a different story.

> Hebrews **11:1** Now faith is the substance of things hoped for, the evidence of things not seen. **2** For by it the elders obtained a *good* testimony. **3** By faith we understand that the worlds were framed by the word of God, so that the things which are seen were not made of things which are visible. (An invisible substance)

> John **1:1** In the beginning was the Word, and the Word was with God, and the Word was God. **2** He was with God in the beginning. **3** Through him all things were made; without him nothing was made that has been made.

God spoke this invisible substance into this dimension and Jesus (called the Word back then) took that substance and began forming this Universe with all its components into existence. The method He used is something we do not completely understand. We also have no understanding of how long this creative process took. All men can do is estimate (meaning guess) at a timeline, which they gleefully do today. I can tell you it took a whole lot longer than 6 days. The account we see in Genesis is a description of God repairing the damage done in Jeremiah 4:23-28 KJV. But we'll see this in more detail later in this chapter that a lot of things took place before the destruction described in Jeremiah.

- Father God spoke the substance of faith into this dimension (Hebrews 11:1-3)

- The Word (Jesus) took that substance and formed everything in this Universe (John 1:1-3)

- That forming took a lot of time and also included the setting in place of all the constellations that tell the story of redemption. This was done long before Adam was created.

- The terraforming of the Earth began. Preparing the land, sea and air so life of any kind could be supported. This would have taken time and lots of it. Time for the foundations to settle, for the echo system to stabilize and flourish

- I know some are thinking this didn't take long as God could just speak and poof it would appear. Scriptures tell a different story about Jesus being a very hands on creator. Very detailed and creative.

Look at what Jesus told Job about the creation process. I say Jesus was speaking to Job because He was the one who did the work of creation (John 1:1-3).

> Job 26:7 He (Jesus) stretches out the north over empty space; *He* hangs the Earth on nothing.

Job was written approximately **4200** years ago. We did not understand the emptiness of space until we went there in the 1960s. We didn't realize that the Earth was hanging on nothing until **185** years ago in 1838 through a discovery by Thomas Henderson and Friedrich Bessel. Yet God knew this because He did it and He told Job.

> Isaiah 40:22 *It is* He (God the Father) who sits above the circle of the Earth,

Men didn't figure out the Earth wasn't flat until the 5th century, but God told Isaiah this **2800** years ago. If we had only believed.

And its inhabitants *are* like grasshoppers, who stretches out the heavens like a curtain, and spreads them out like a tent to dwell in. (This is in reference to the stars, planets and galaxies)

> Isaiah 40:25 "To whom then will you liken Me, Or *to whom* shall I be equal?" says the Holy One.

Isaiah 40:26 Lift up your eyes on high, and see who has created these *things, w*ho brings out their host by number (The Stars); He calls them all by name, by the greatness of His might and the strength of *His* power; Not one is missing.

God controls the planets, stars and constellation movements. This was observed first by Copernicus in the 1500s and was confirmed later by science. Astronomers have observed that every planet goes into **Retrograde** (explained more in depth later in chapter The Proof in the Stars) at least once per year. This is a recognizable resetting of the planets orbital track if one has the eyes to see it. This is meaningful because it is not done by accident (The Big Bang Theory tells us everything is done by accident) if it occurs regularly for each planet.

Retrograde looks like the planet is moving on its course as it normally does. Then it slows down and eventually stops. After this it appears to move backward on its orbital course for a bit. Next it looks like it is slowing down and stopping again. After this it will reverse into its normal speed and direction. From our position on Earth, the retrograde path of the planet is sometimes referred to as a 'halo' or 'crowning' effect. The Retrograde of the planet Jupiter (it went into retrograde 3 times in less than a year) caught the attention of the Magi and inspired their trip to Jerusalem (also explained later in Chapter 6: The Proof in the Stars). But that's not the whole story. Jupiter was called the King Planet back then.

Jupiter, while in retrograde, haloed the distant star named Regulus (back then it was called the Little King) and it did this three times in the center of the constellation of Leo. Retrograde usually occurs in open space, and that's another reason the Magi noticed the difference. So the King Planet haloed the Little King star Regulus while in the center of the Leo constellation. It did this 3 times in less than a year. No wonder the Magi hightailed it to Jerusalem to honor the new King of Israel. Retrograde shows us plainly that there is intelligent control involved with the movement of the planets in our solar system, which common sense tells us someone is in control. None of it is by accident, as the Intellectual Elites (as Graham Hancock likes to call them) would have us believe with The Big Bang Theory.

Jesus continues with Job here.

> Job 38:4 "Where were you when I laid the foundations of the Earth?
>
> Tell *Me,* if you have understanding.
>
> 5 Who determined its measurements? Surely you know! Or who stretched the line upon it?
>
> 6 To what were its foundations fastened? Or who laid its cornerstone,
>
> 8 Or *who* shut in the sea with doors, when it burst forth *and* issued from the womb;
>
> 9 When I made the clouds its garment, and thick darkness its swaddling band;
>
> 10 When I fixed My limit for it, and set bars and doors;
>
> 11 When I said, 'This far you may come, but no farther, and here your proud waves must stop!'
>
> Isaiah 40:12 Who has measured the waters in the hollow of His hand, Measured heaven with a span and calculated the dust of the Earth in a measure? Weighed the mountains in scales and the hills in a balance?

Jesus is telling us through Job and Isaiah, here is a detailed summary of some of the things He did when He was in the process of creating just the Earth. Again, we see the information spread over multiple books of the Bible. Look at all the different steps Jesus cited here. This was hands-on work in forming these physical features out of the substance of faith. He did not just speak these things into existence, even though He could have. This took time and a lot of it. It was a very hands-on creation, as described in Job and Isaiah.

> Genesis 1:1-3
>
> **1** In the beginning God created the heaven and the Earth.

Here in verse one the word '**created**' is translated from the Hebrew word **baw-raw** which means to **create out of nothing**. This gives us more information confirming that when God started this creation process nothing was there. Then God spoke the substance of faith into this vast empty space.

> Isaiah 45:18 For thus saith the Lord that created the heavens; God himself that formed the Earth and made it; he hath established it, he created it **not in vain**, he formed it to be inhabited: I am the Lord; and there is none else.

Note, the Hebrew word **tohu means 'empty'**, but here it is translated in vain. Why? If you change the verse to the proper meaning you get.

> Isaiah 45:18 For thus saith the Lord that created the heavens; God himself that formed the Earth and made it; he hath established it, he created it **not empty**, he formed it to be inhabited: I am the Lord; and there is none else.

So, the Earth and heavens were created by God and they were ready for habitation in Genesis 1:1, and according to Isaiah 45:18 the Earth was not **empty.** As you'll see later in this chapter, God knew He was going to put Lucifer in charge as Covering Cherub (Ezekiel 28:14). Therefore, I believe the Earth was fully inhabited soon after creation and before Lucifer took over. This knowledge gives us one more reason to believe that this is where the *TIME GAP occurs.*

Now we come to:

> Genesis 1:**2** And the Earth was without form, and void; and darkness was upon the face of the deep. And the Spirit of God moved upon the face of the waters.

Alright, we see here that something happened between these two verses and it's quite a change. The Earth goes from **perfectly habitable** and **not empty** (Genesis 1:1; Isaiah 45:18) to without form and void, covered in water, and totally in the dark. That's a big change and it involves time and some event or events we at this point know nothing about.

I believe that the Bible is the "true Word of God." It has to be all true or nothing is true. So, why doesn't Genesis' first two verses make sense? Well, when in doubt, go back to the original language and in this case, it is Hebrew. In Genesis 1:2, the word that is translated **was** in English actually means **became** in Hebrew. That's right, the Hebrew word **hayah** means **became** in English. It was translated as became **67** other times in the Bible (i.e. Genesis 2:7; 19:26; 20:12; 24:67), but not in Genesis 1:2. Also, Genesis 1:2 has the English words '**without form and void**' in Hebrew they are **tohu va bohu** and mean '**waste and empty**'. So it seems that a very large error has occurred (maybe accidental or intentional). When translated properly as **became waste and empty**, Genesis 1:2 lines up perfectly with the Jeremiah 4:23-28 account.

Genesis 1:2 should have read: 'And the Earth **became waste and empty;** and darkness was upon the face of the deep. And the Spirit of God moved upon the face of the waters.' Now when we bring in Jeremiah, the mystery deepens:

Jeremiah 4:**23** I beheld the Earth, and, lo, it was without form, and void; and the heavens, and they had no light. (Here, these are the same Hebrew words as Genesis 1:2 **tohu va bohu** and mean '**waste and empty**' not void)

Jeremiah 4:**23** should read 'I beheld the Earth, and, lo, it was **waste and empty;** and the heavens, and they had no light.' This translation correction makes it clear the event in Jeremiah's vision was the cause of the dramatic change described in Genesis 1:2.

Now, these mistranslations seem a bit intentional. God was very exact in Isaiah 45:18, saying He created it **not empty**, which indicates the Earth was populated when He finished. But it was changed to **not in vain**, which doesn't really say anything. When we add these multiple mistranslations in Genesis 1:2 from 'the Earth **became waste and empty**'; (a deliberate statement full of meaning) to 'the Earth **was without form, and void**' (which is an innocuous phrase). This deception continues with the changes to Jeremiah 4:23 where it is changed from 'I beheld the Earth, and, lo, it was **waste and empty**' to 'I beheld the Earth, and, lo, it was **without form, and void**'; another vague statement. I believe that the devil, who is the King of Deceivers, is deliberately trying to confuse and mislead the reader.

This is the event Jeremiah witnessed in his vision:

> Jeremiah 4:**24** I beheld the mountains, and, lo, they trembled, and all the hills moved lightly. **25** I beheld, and, lo, there was no man, and all the birds of the heavens were fled. **26** I beheld, and, lo, the fruitful place was a wilderness, and all the cities thereof were broken down at

the presence of the Lord, and by his fierce anger. **27** For thus hath the Lord said, The whole land shall be desolate; yet will I not make a full end. **28** For this shall the Earth mourn, and the heavens above be black; because I have spoken it, I have purposed it, and will not repent, neither will I turn back from it.

2 Peter 3:6 Whereby the world that then was, being overflowed with water, perished:

By matching these two verses, before the mistranslations appeared, God was leading us from Genesis to Jeremiah for additional information on what happened and why. Jeremiah 4:28 explains the darkness part of Genesis 1:2. Simple, God turned the lights of the Universe off for some reason. 2 Peter 3:6 confirms the flood and that the Earth perished. Remember, the vegetation, animals and man survived Noah's flood. Notice now that Jeremiah 4 verses 23 and 28 match the corrected statement in Genesis 1:2, therefore the verses in-between in Jeremiah add to the story. So when God finished His creation, the Earth was perfect and ready for habitation. Isaiah added to this that it was Not Empty. The inference therefore is that the Earth was flourishing in vegetation, animals and people. Then, Jeremiah's vision showed us how it became waste, empty and flooded with absolutely no light. So, we know God caused this event but we don't know why yet.

Let's see if the New Testament can add any more information:

Matthew 13:35 That it might be fulfilled which was spoken by the prophet, saying, I will open my mouth in parables; I will utter things which have been kept secret from the **foundation** of the world. (Does this mean from the original foundation setting that Job was told about (Job 38:4-6)?)

Turns out **no**. The word translated foundation here is the Greek word **KATABOLE**, which translates to '**cast or throw down**'.

Matthew 13:35 That it might be fulfilled which was spoken by the prophet, saying, I will open my mouth in parables; I will utter things which have been kept secret from the **overthrow** of the world.

Luke 11:50 That the blood of all the prophets, which was shed from the **overthrow** of the world, may be required of this generation; **(I made the correction in this verse because it was the same Greek word KATABOLE was also mistranslated here as foundation)**

Hebrews 4:3 For we which have believed do enter into rest, as he said, As I have sworn in my wrath, if they shall enter into my rest: although the works were finished from the **foundation** of the world.

Again, here in Hebrews 4:3, we have another mistranslation. The Greek words **KATABOLE KOSMOU** mean **the disruption or casting down of the social system**. These two words were **translated as Foundation**. Also, here we learn this was said at a time when God was angry. We know that Jeremiah 4:26 tells us that God was fiercely angry, and that's when He destroyed that world.

So then, Hebrews 4:3 should have been translated: For we which have believed do enter into rest, as he said, As I have sworn in my wrath, if they shall enter into my rest: although the works were finished from the **casting down of the social system** of the world.

Revelation 13:8 And all that dwell upon the Earth shall worship him, whose names are not written in the book of life of the Lamb slain from the **foundation** of the world.

Again, the word translated foundation here is the same Greek word **KATABOLE** which (as you know by now) equals to **cast or throw down**.

It should have read; Revelation 13:8 And all that dwell upon the Earth shall worship him, whose names are not written in the book of life of the Lamb slain from the **overthrow** of the world.

Revelation 17:8 The beast that thou sawest was, and is not; and shall ascend out of the bottomless pit, and go into perdition: and they that dwell on the Earth shall wonder, whose names were not written in the book of life from the **foundation** of the world, when they behold the beast that was, and is not, and yet is.

Revelation 17:8 should have read; The beast that thou sawest was, and is not; and shall ascend out of the bottomless pit, and go into perdition: and they that dwell on the Earth shall wonder, whose names were not written in the book of life from the **overthrow** of the world, when they behold the beast that was, and is not, and yet is.

These errors in translation tend to make me think someone is trying consistently to hide or camouflage the same truth. That truth being there was an ancient civilization here on Earth before Adam and it was **overthrown by God**. It strikes me to be a very deliberate and coordinated effort to consistently make the same mistake for one particular word and phrase. This consistency makes me lean more to believing the GAP THEORY than disbelieving it. I believe God was trying to tell the truth and someone else is trying to cover it up. The other interesting truth here is that according to Hebrews 4:3; Revelation 13:8; 17:8 the **Book of Life** was written after the **overthrow** of Lucifer, his rebellion, and his world. That event in our distant past was also the start of this Dispensation of God's creation process, which includes this version of man in Adam. He was created in the image of God as a three part being.

For now let's continue with the Genesis story.

> Genesis 1:**3** And God said, Let there be light: and there was light.

In verse 3, we see God turning the lights back on. God is just speaking here, using His power to reverse what He did in Jeremiah 4:28. Or did He? We're made in His image and we participate in wisecracks (at least I do) a lot or at least once in a while. So muse about it a bit. He's been away from this for some time. Jesus and the Holy Spirit are there waiting for Him. So He joins them with a huge smile, arms raised and His booming voice shouts "Let there be light" and light appears all around. But it's still not from the sun or stars. It's His Glory shining and filling the area. Remember Revelation 21:23 that in New Jerusalem, there is no need for the sun and stars to produce light, because the light comes just from the Glory of His presence. This was only the **first day**. He didn't recreate the sun and stars until day four.

Day Four

> Genesis 1:**14** And God said, Let there be lights in the firmament of the heaven to divide the day from the night; and let them be for signs, and for seasons, and for days, and years: **15** And let them be for lights in the firmament of the heaven to give light upon the Earth: and it was so.
>
> **16** And God made two great lights; the greater light to rule the day, and the lesser light to rule the night: he made the stars also. **17** And God set them in the firmament of the heaven to give light upon the Earth, **18** And to rule

over the day and over the night, and to divide the light from the darkness: and God saw that it was good. **19** And the evening and the morning were the fourth day.

On day four, God obviously refined the lights and repaired the damage that Jeremiah witnessed in his vision. Now we've seen why Genesis 1:2 doesn't line up with Genesis 1:1 and Isaiah. Because it had been mistranslated. One group of words changed the entire meaning of that verse and it affected many others. Revelation 12:9 tells that Satan deceives the whole world and this is only one example of that behavior. And I believe the great deceiver Satan was at work here in the most subtle and diabolical way. By changing just one group of words in two different books of the Bible from **became waste and empty** (also hiding his failure) to **was without form, and void.** He has caused confusion down through the centuries. This change caused people to believe there was only one flood and that nothing existed before Adam and Eve. By doing this, he also opened the door for speculations like Evolution and The Big Bang Theories. The ramifications from that one phrase being changed in several different books of the Bible are astounding. Truly, Satan is the King of Deceivers and the Father of Lies (Revelation 12:9; John 8:44).

This enlightens us that Satan is an intelligent spirit being who should not be ignored nor taken lightly. Think about what he brought about here by making these slight changes:

1. He hid his failure

2. Caused believers to be unaware of his reign here before Adam

3. Camouflaged God dealing with his sin using the First Flood (pre-Adam)

4. He was then able to deceive the followers of God (the Church) into believing everything started with Adam (nothing existed before 6000 years ago and no longer).

5. This then allowed Satan to introduce his false theories of Evolution and Big Bang

6. As time progressed he had Christians defending the 6000 year creation timeline while fighting real physical fossilized archeological and scientific evidence. All non-Christians have to do is point to the museum's Dino-bones along with the scientific proof that it takes

at least 10,000 years to form a fossil. The Christian argument then sounded foolish.

7. To put icing on the cake all Satan had to do was keep whispering that the Bible was not accurate and just full of fairytales for weak minded people who need a crutch. Satan is not and never has been the friend of humans and especially Christians and Jews.

> Ephesians 6:12 For we wrestle not against flesh and blood, but against principalities, against powers, against the rulers of the darkness of this world, against spiritual wickedness in high places.

Unfortunately, because he works from the shadows of another dimension, humans are usually not aware of his nor his minion's presence. We walk with open eyes, but blindly step into his traps much to our dismay and regret. He is angry at God because he was defeated in his rebellion, as you'll see later in this chapter. God, through that defeat, removed him from his earthly throne. Satan wants to get even with God. He thinks he is better than God and definitely far superior to the humans God chose to put in his place. I imagine that after his defeat he watched as everything he had created was destroyed (Jeremiah 4:23-28). God had destroyed his creation and Satan was mad beyond reason. But he was powerless at that point and had to wait until God made His next move.

He would have skulked around in the dark for thousands of Earth years, brooding over his revenge. Then, all of a sudden, the lights came back on. God was back. Time to pay attention he would have probably thought. Watching as God removed the waters from the once dry land of Earth. Resetting the stars, planets and recreated the sun. The dry land was pretty much as before except all of Satan's beautiful cities were in ruins and covered in mud for the most part. God had just spoke and the water had immediately flowed away (Genesis 1:9-10). Anger would probably have flared within him as he looked at the ruins of his once flourishing civilization. His creation, his kingdom, now lay in ruins, and God was to blame. He would have vowed revenge, but didn't quite know how to proceed at that moment. Satan watched God work quickly and then he heard God say:

> Genesis 1:26 And God said, Let us make man in our image, after our likeness: and let them have dominion over the fish of the sea, and over the fowl of the air, and

over the cattle, and over all the Earth, and over every creeping thing that creepeth upon the Earth.

Anger would have raged in Satan when he heard that God was going to create a man again and give them his kingdom. But he probably recognized this was also an opportunity. The weakness in God's plan he had been watching for. After all, men weren't very special nor intelligent when he reigned over them. So, he watched God create this new man who would rule his kingdom in his stead.

> Genesis 2:7 And the Lord God formed man of the dust of the ground, and breathed into his nostrils the breath of life; and man became a living soul.

Satan recognized something was different this time from the original creation. After all, he had watched the original creation with the other angels.

> Job 38:**6** Whereupon are the foundations thereof fastened? Or who laid the corner stone thereof;
>
> **7** When the morning stars sang together, and all the sons of God shouted for joy?

They were all witnesses to the creation of Earth, animals and man. The last time God created a man, He stopped at forming him from the Earth and there were several varieties, but they functioned okay, just like every other animal. (There is archeological evidence that 8 different types of Hominids (as scientist like to call them, not human but sort of close) existed on Earth at the same time in the Earth's past.) However, this time there was only one version, and God breathed into this man, creating a spirit being which was covered in a fleshly body. This was new.

Then God created the Garden of Eden and placed Adam in it. Genesis 2:8-14 KJV. Once Adam was in the Garden God showed him around and then gave him only one rule.

> Genesis 2:**16** And the Lord God commanded the man, saying, Of every tree of the garden thou mayest freely eat: **17** But of the Tree of the Knowledge of Good and Evil, thou shalt not eat of it: for in the day that thou eatest thereof thou shalt surely die. (So don't eat of the Tree of Knowledge of Good and Evil. If he does he will die that day. Now, God was not talking about Adam dying physically, but that the spirit within him would die.)

Then, God made every animal out of the ground and brought them to Adam and he named them all (Genesis 2:18-20). No suitable mate was found for Adam. So, God put Adam to sleep and removed one of his ribs. From this rib, God formed woman. Because she was not directly formed from the ground, but from Adam's own blood, bone and flesh, part of his spirit transferred to her in this process. This is what made this latest and last version of man so different, and why God didn't have to breathe His spirit into the woman as well. Think about this. To create a baby, the sperm (seed of the man) enters the womb of the woman, and there that seed is covered with flesh, blood and bone before it is born. The baby has all three parts, spirit from the seed of man, a body, blood and bone and a mind. A three part being Spirit, Body and Soul or mind. This spirit does not know God.

By obeying Satan instead of God, Adam transferred his rulership of the Earth back to Satan. From that point to this, Satan has been the ruler of this Earth again. The reason he hates men so much is that part of the curse God put on man for disobedience was as follows:

> Genesis 3:14 And the Lord God said unto the serpent, Because thou hast done this, thou art cursed above all cattle, and above every beast of the field; upon thy belly shalt thou go, and dust shalt thou eat all the days of thy life: 15 And I will put enmity between thee and the woman, and between thy seed and her seed; it shall bruise thy head, and thou shalt bruise his heel.

This is a dual curse here: one part for the serpent, and the other part for the devil. In part, this is why Satan hates humans so much and why he is attacking us and trying to kill us at every opportunity. He's proud, angry and vengeful and since he can't attack God he's more than happy to take his anger out on us.

We can conclude then that there was a civilization populated by men (not quite the same as Adam) and animals before Adam on Earth. Also something happened that angered God so much He destroyed everything with a catastrophic flood and then turned the lights of the Universe off. The questions explode off the page now. What happened, can we determine when, and can this be proven further through scripture, archeology and science? The short answer again is Yes.

***

The Reason for this Destruction

> 2 Peter 3:5 For this they willingly are ignorant of, that by the word of God the heavens were of old, and the Earth standing out of the water and in the water: 6 Whereby the world that then was, being overflowed with water, perished:

This is a reference to Lucifer's civilization, not Noah's, and today the scriptures referring to this time are being ignored. I say ignored, because in our day and age the truth of the scriptures are not valued as they once were. This is being done today despite the abundant archeological and scientific evidence, which prove the validity of these scriptures. Therefore we are willingly ignorant by **simply accepting** what our teachers and experts of the world (the Intellectual Elites as Graham Hancock likes to call them) are telling us without checking the facts for ourselves.

Now we know this happened before Adam, but why did God do this? And in that question lies the Gap Theory. A period of time when Lucifer reigned here on Earth many thousands of years before Adam and Eve were created. The Genesis story is the beginning of this current dispensation of creation through **intentional design and not evolution**. This new man was given something that was not present in the men who apparently (according to scripture Jeremiah 4:25) lived under Lucifer's reign and that difference was an eternal spirit.

> Genesis 1:26 And God said, Let us make man in our image, after our likeness: (further description found in Genesis 2:7) And the Lord God formed man of the dust of the ground, (just like the animals and when animals die they return to the dust) and then God breathed into his nostrils the breath of life; and man became a living soul. (Please realize that the animals were formed and living without God having to breathe life into them. God is imparting His eternal spirit here but only to man and after that Adam lived.)

We are made very differently from the animals. We are a three part being, body, mind and eternal spirit just like the Godhead. It is my assumption that the men before Adam did not have an eternal spirit. Now the reason for this assumption is because God is a just God and He knew that Lucifer would eventually rebel and also he would do a terrible job in his rule over Earth. Knowing this fact Father God would never have intentionally condemned millions of men to eternal damnation. Not without giving them a chance for saving their spirits, if they had a spirit, just to test Lucifer and the angelic host.

Also, keep in mind that the Lamb's Book of Life was started after the overthrow of Lucifer's kingdom (Hebrews 4:3; Revelation 13:8; 17:8). Hell was created only for the Devil and his angels (Matthew 25:41), man was never intended to go there. Men have to freely choose their eternal destination. In our justice system, ignorance of a law is not a defense. The same applies to God's laws. Keep this in mind that every higher spirit being had to make a free will choice, to follow God or not. Remember, most of the angels chose willingly to follow God. This was the angels' chance to choose to follow God or not. So, my assumption stands: those men back then would have been just as the animals were without an eternal spirit being. When they passed away, they would have just returned to the dust of the Earth as the animals do.

> 2 Corinthians 5:**5** Now he that hath wrought us for the selfsame thing is God, who also hath given unto us the earnest of the Spirit. **6** Therefore we are always confident, knowing that, whilst we are at home in the body, we are absent from the Lord: **7** (For we walk by faith, not by sight :) **8** We are confident, I say, and willing rather to be absent from the body, and to be present with the Lord.

Now our eternal spirit being lives in our body and we have a mind, but when we humans pass away, our bodies go back to the ground, just like the animals. But our spirit being returns to the spirit realm. If we are saved in Jesus, we go to be with him, however if we are not saved, our spirit goes to eternal damnation. This is just a fact, like it or not, believe it or not. Our lives are for one purpose ultimately, and that is to find God and then choose to follow Him through Jesus or not. Once you understand that, life becomes a lot simpler.

> Genesis 1:**26** and let them have dominion over the fish of the sea, and over the fowl of the air, and over the cattle, and over all the Earth, and over every creeping thing that crept upon the Earth. **27** So God created man in his own image, in the image of God He created him; male and female He created them. **28** And God blessed them, and God said unto them, Be fruitful, and multiply, and **replenish the Earth**, and subdue it: and have dominion

over the fish of the sea, and over the fowl of the air, and over every living thing that moveth upon the Earth.

Please notice here that God did not end His statement at "multiply and fill the Earth", but He said multiply and **replenish** the Earth, indicating there were men on Earth before Adam to **replace**. So, the question now arises as to when and why this happened. We have to go back to scripture to determine those answers, and we start with having a look at the villain in this story, Lucifer.

The instigating event that triggered all of this and this new Dispensation since Adam can be narrowed down to one thing: when God created Lucifer.

***

Lucifer was Satan's name before he rebelled:

> Ezekiel 28:12 '… Thou were the seal of perfection, full of wisdom, and perfect in beauty. (Not the human king of Tyre as some have taught)

> Ezekiel 28:13 'Thou hast been in Eden the Garden of God; (This Garden was in Heaven before Adam and Eve), every precious stone was thy covering, the Sardius, Topaz, and the Diamond, the Beryl, the Onyx, and the Jasper, the Sapphire, the Emerald, and the Carbuncle, and Gold: the workmanship of thy taberets and of thy pipes was prepared in thee in the day thou wast created.

> Ezekiel 28:14 'Thou art the anointed Cherub that covereth; (Lucifer is an angelic Cherubim and here he's given a special position. He was to rule the Earth and guide them to know about and worship God.) and I have set thee so; (God put Lucifer in charge the same way he put Adam in charge.) thou wast upon the holy mountain of God; thou has walked up and down in the midst of the stones of fire.

> Ezekiel 28:15 Thou wast perfect in thy ways from the day that thou wast created, till iniquity was found in thee.

(This is a description of Lucifer before he fell and rebelled. Remember he was already fallen before he tempted Eve in the Garden of Eden. Therefore this occurred before the Genesis story.)

How ruling Earth changed Lucifer

So, as we have just seen when Lucifer was given the post of Covering Cherub for the Earth and at that moment, he was perfect in all his ways with no sin. Otherwise, he could not have walked on the Holy Mountain of God, nor be in God's presence, because sin cannot be in close proximity to God and live. However, as we know over a long period of absence accompanied by pride in your great successes and riches, one can become indifferent to family, friends, spouses and bosses. One can even become angry at them when they criticize your results or future plans. You begin to think you and only you know best, and that is the problem I believe Lucifer found himself in after ruling on Earth for many thousands of years. He wanted to do things his way, and not God's way, and resented any attempts at correction.

Isaiah 14:12 'How art thou fallen from heaven, O Lucifer, son of the morning! How art thou cut down to the ground, which did weaken the nations.

(Nations that he had developed by the way and again remember Lucifer rebelled before Adam and Eve came into being. So this is telling us these were nations that existed before Adam and the Genesis story.)

Ezekiel 28:16 By the multitude of thy merchandise

(Lucifer's accumulated wealth made him very proud.)

Ezekiel 28:5 By thy great wisdom and by thy traffick hast thou increased thy riches, and thine heart is lifted up because of thy riches:

(So we learn that it was not only his beauty, but also his great wealth that led Lucifer to be seriously full of himself and full of pride at what he had accomplished here on Earth. So much so he began to think he was like God.)

Ezekiel 28:4 With thy wisdom and with thine understanding thou hast gotten thee riches, and hast gotten gold and silver into thy treasures:

(He used the wisdom God gave him to make himself rich.)

Ezekiel 28:17 Thou heart was lifted up because of thy beauty, thou hast corrupted thy wisdom by the reason of thy brightness.

Isaiah 14:13 'For thou hast said in thine heart, I will ascend into heaven,

(This is telling us he was not in heaven but to accomplish his rebellion he had to ascend from where he was on Earth to accomplish throwing God off His throne and taking God's place as King.)

I will exalt my throne above the stars of God: I will sit also upon the mount of the congregation, in the sides of the north:

Isaiah 14:14 I will ascend above the heights of the clouds; I will be like the most high.

(What happened when Lucifer rebelled? Well one third of the angels chose to follow him in a war to overthrow God in heaven. Archangel Michael and the rest of the angels fought against them and won. We don't know how long this took, but we do know it was before Adam. The Earth and its inhabitants at the time followed Lucifer and we see in the following verses what happened to them, but first let's look at how Lucifer ruled Earth.)

How Lucifer ruled on Earth

Parts of the first 10 verses of Ezekiel 28 apply to a human king and the spirit king of Tyre. As we see in Daniel 10:13; 20-21, there are human and spirit rulers associated with various areas and kingdoms on Earth. Daniel's case tells us of the spirit princes of Persia and Greece resisting Daniel's angel and Michael. Here in Tyre, the same principal applies, because God is consistent, and so is the Devil.

> Ezekiel 28:2 Son of man, say unto the prince of Tyre (this I believe is also to the spirit prince of Tyre) Thus saith the Lord God; Because thine heart is lifted up, and thou hast said, I am a God, I sit in the seat of God, in the midst of the seas; yet thou art a man, and not God, though thou set thine heart as the heart of God:

> (This is a duel statement it can apply to Satan and the Human King. These verses are also historic, before Adam, current day of that time, and future which involves Satan's defeat at Armageddon and being chained in the pit when Jesus returns. This mirrors Revelation for Past, Present and Future events depicted.)

Ezekiel 28:3 Behold, thou art wiser than Daniel; there is no secret that they can hide from thee; (He is not talking about a human here. Satan has spirits with everyone and they report back to him about us so he can accuse us before God. (Revelation 12:9-10)

Ezekiel 28:4 With thy wisdom and with thine understanding thou hast gotten thee riches, and hast gotten gold and silver into thy treasures:

Ezekiel 28:5 By thy great wisdom and by thy traffick (commercial Trade) hast thou increased thy riches, and thine heart is lifted up because of thy riches:

(So we learn that it was not only his beauty, but also his great wealth that led Lucifer to be seriously full of himself and full of pride at what he had accomplished here on Earth. So much so he began to think he was God. We know this is speaking to Lucifer because the word Traffick (meaning commercial trade) and reference to his great wisdom.)

Ezekiel 28:16 …thy have filled the midst of thee with violence, and thou hast sinned: therefore I will cast thee as profane out of the mountain of God: and I will destroy thee, O covering Cherub, from the midst of the stones of fire.

Isaiah 14:6 He who smote the people in wrath with a continual stroke, he that ruled the nations in anger…

(So, he did rule people and nations unfettered and in anger for a time in the Earth's past before Adam.)

Ezekiel 28:18 Thou hast defiled thy sanctuaries by the multitude of thine iniquities, by the iniquity of thy traffick; therefore will I bring forth a fire from the midst of thee, it shall devour thee, and I will bring thee to ashes upon the Earth in the sight of all them that behold thee.

Jeremiah 4:22 'For my people (humans (hominids) under Lucifer) are foolish, they have not known Me; they are silly children, and they have no understanding: they are wise to do evil, but to do good they have no knowledge.'

(We see here how poor of a job Lucifer actually did in teaching the people of the Earth at that time about God and His ways. Now we are about to see what happened to the Earth after Lucifer's defeated rebellion.)

What Happened to Earth because of Lucifer

We've seen these scriptures before, but it is here that they occur in Lucifer's timeline and takes place after Lucifer's rebellion has been put down.

Jeremiah 4:23 'I beheld the Earth, and, it was without form, and void; *(sound familiar?)* Genesis 1:2) and the heavens, and they had no light.

(This tells us that the lights of the Universe had turned off. Think about it who else but God has that kind of power?)

Jeremiah 4:24 'I beheld the mountains, and, lo, they trembled, and all the hills moved lightly. *(This is telling us why God had to recreate some of the mountains in the Genesis creation story because they were destroyed here.)*

Jeremiah 4:25 'I beheld, and, lo, there was no man, and all the birds of heaven were fled.

(So there were men but not anymore, there were birds and animals but all are gone).

Jeremiah 4:26 'I beheld, and, lo, the fruitful place was a wilderness, and all the cities thereof were broken down at the presence of the Lord, and by His fierce anger.

(This shows us that in His great anger God Himself put judgment on the despicable world Lucifer had created. God Himself destroyed all the cities that had existed under Lucifer and there is plenty of Archaeological evidence of this destruction that we will discuss later.)

Jeremiah 4:27 'For thus hath the Lord said, the whole land shall be desolate; yet I will not make a full end.

Jeremiah 4:28 For this shall the Earth mourn, and the heavens above be black; because I have spoken it, I have purposed it, and will not repent, neither will I turn back from it.

(Here we see in this verse the proof from God Himself what He did in His Judgment of Lucifer's world. God turned the lights of the Universe off personally, and the Genesis story is just telling us how He turned them back on. My assumption

is that he had to recreate the suns and stars in order to do this.)

Hebrews 10:31 It is a fearful thing to fall into the hands of the living God.

Hebrews 4:3 For we which have believed do enter into rest, as he said, As I have sworn in my wrath (Now we know that God was only mad enough to destroy the whole world utterly once and that was after Lucifer was defeated in his rebellion), if they shall enter into my rest: although the works were finished from **the casting down of the social system of the world**.

(The mistranslation here was of the Greek words **katabole kosmou** which equal - **the disruption or casting down of the social system**. Once corrected the scripture becomes clearer. However these Greek words had been once again mistranslated as **foundation**. God was so mad at what Lucifer had created that He knew He had to start over. He also knew this would come and that is the reason He created the pre-Adamic men without an eternal spirit.)

Revelation 13:7 And it was given unto him to make war with the saints, and to overcome them: and power was given him over all kindreds, and tongues, and nations. **8** And all that dwell upon the Earth shall worship him, whose names are not written in the book of life of the Lamb slain from the **overthrow** (not foundation) of the world. **9** If any man have an ear, let him hear.

(Once we correct the mistranslation of the Greek word **katabole** from "**foundation**" to the proper meaning "**to cast or throw down**" we have a better understanding of the whole story the word is telling the believers. You see this scripture is informing us of when the Godhead initiated their plan for the redemptive sacrifice of Jesus. The Lamb slain from the **overthrow** of Lucifer's world Revelation 13:7. This is also showing us at what time God looked into the future and wrote down the names of all who will believe in Jesus in His Book of Life. Here is where predestination started for the future. This was done after Lucifer's defeat and the utter destruction of the world he had developed, before Adam and Eve.)

Matthew 13:35 That it might be fulfilled which was spoken by the prophet, saying, I will open my mouth in parables; I will utter things which have been kept secret from the overthrow of the world.

(Jesus was telling them that the secrets were kept since Lucifer's world was overthrown completely by God's Judgment on it. This is not Noah's world because everything then was not destroyed as it was with Lucifer's social system back then. Apparently in God's Judgment there was no way to correct the damage Lucifer had done so he wiped it all out.)

God's Final Plan for Satan

Ezekiel 28:6 Therefore thus saith the Lord God;

Ezekiel 28:7 *(Again we see Present (for the time it was originally given), and Future even to our time in 2023)* Behold, therefore I will bring strangers upon thee, the terrible of the nations:

(For the Future side of this prophecy Satan will be backing the Anti-Christ in the Tribulation, but he won't control the whole world. God will bring an Arab Alliance and the 200 million strong Asian army against him at Armageddon and that is when Christ returns and we return with Him as well as the angels)

And they shall draw their swords against the beauty of thy wisdom, and they shall defile thy brightness.

Ezekiel 28:17 Thine heart was lifted up because of thy beauty, thou hast corrupted thy wisdom by reason of thy brightness: I will cast thee to the ground, I will lay thee before kings, that they may behold thee.

(This takes place after Armageddon.)

Ezekiel 28:8 They shall bring thee down to the pit,

(Now here God is speaking to Satan's fate in our future beyond 2023 because Satan is the only one taken to the Pit.)

Revelation 9:1 And the fifth angel sounded, and I saw a star fall from heaven unto the Earth: and to him was given the key of the bottomless pit.

Revelation 9:2 And he opened the bottomless pit; and there arose a smoke out of the pit, as the smoke of a great furnace; and the sun and the air were darkened by reason of the smoke of the pit.

(This is when the bottomless pit leading to hell is opened to release the locusts who are led by the angel Abbaddon. They will sting and torment all men who are not one of the 144,000 Jewish evangelists marked by God. This will be done for the first five months of the Tribulation. I just wanted to show you where this pit goes to and that the pit has to be opened before the devil is chained to it.)

Revelation 20:**1** And I saw an angel come down from heaven, having the key of the bottomless pit and a great chain in his hand. **2** And he laid hold on the dragon, that old serpent, which is the Devil, and Satan, and bound him a thousand years, **3** And cast him into the bottomless pit, and shut him up, and set a seal upon him, that he should deceive the nations no more, till the thousand years should be fulfilled: and after that he must be loosed a little season.

(Satan will spend the Millennium chained to the side of the bottomless pit. He is also gagged so he cannot speak to anyone or tempt anyone during this time period.)

Isaiah 14:**15** Yet thou shalt be brought down to hell, to the sides of the pit. **16** They that see thee shall narrowly look upon thee, and consider thee, saying, "Is this the man that made the Earth to tremble, that did shake kingdoms; **17** That made the world as a wilderness, and destroyed the cities thereof; that opened not the house of his prisoners?"

(Notice that Isaiah has been inspired by God in this description of the world as a wilderness to tie these verses back to Jeremiah 4:26, which in turn ties them back to Lucifer's world before Adam)

*Isaiah 14:***18** All the kings of the nations, even all of them, lie in glory, every one in his own house. **19** But thou art cast out of thy grave like an abominable branch, and as the raiment of those that are slain, thrust through with a sword, that go down to the stones of the pit; as a carcass trodden under feet.

Revelation 20:**7** And when the thousand years are expired, Satan shall be loosed out of his prison, **8** And shall go out to deceive the nations which are in the four quarters of the Earth, Gog, and Magog, to gather them together to battle: the number of whom is as the sand of the sea. **9** And they went up on the breadth of the Earth, and compassed the camp of the saints about, and the beloved city: and fire came down from God out of heaven, and devoured them. **10** And the devil that deceived them was cast into the lake of fire and brimstone, where the beast and the false prophet are, and shall be tormented day and night for ever and ever.

(And I believe that in time after all have been judged at the White Throne Judgment and Satan has been tormented in the Lake of Fire for that period of time God will complete the following verses in front of all.)

The following is a description of how fire is directed against Satan's army at the end of the Millennium. God's army is composed of every believer in Christ. It is an immortal army that is directly guided by Jesus. The result will be that everything before them is consumed by the fire from God. God must feel that He again must start His recreation process for the Earth over again. He's not starting totally over this time, because all the believers in Jesus who were born to human mothers during the Millennium would have needed to choose Jesus during that time. If they came to faith in Jesus and followed Him during the Millennium, they would have probably sought refuge in Jerusalem during this attack. Therefore, they would still be alive after God's army, and the fire defeated and consumed Satan's forces in this battle. So, these natural people would be able to replenish the human population on Earth with their children when God will have recreated the Earth after Satan has finally been defeated in this final battle at the end of the Millennium. Joel gives us a description of that event:

Joel 2:**1** Blow ye the trumpet in Zion, and sound an alarm in my holy mountain: let all the inhabitants of the land tremble: for the day of the Lord cometh, for it is nigh at hand;

2 A day of darkness and of gloominess, a day of clouds and of thick darkness, as the morning spread upon the mountains: a great people and a strong; there hath not been ever the like, neither shall be any more after it, even to the years of many generations. **3** A fire devoureth before them; and behind them a flame burneth: the land is as the garden of Eden before them, and behind them a desolate wilderness; yea, and nothing shall escape them. **4** The appearance of them is as the appearance of horses; and as horsemen, so shall they run. **5** Like the noise of chariots on the tops of mountains shall they leap, like the noise of a flame of fire that devoureth the stubble, as a strong people set in battle array.

6 Before their face the people shall be much pained: all faces shall gather blackness. **7** They shall run like mighty men; they shall climb the wall like men of war; and they shall march every one on his ways, and they shall not break their ranks: **8** Neither shall one thrust another; they shall walk every one in his path: and when they fall upon the sword, they shall not be wounded. **9** They shall run to and fro in the city; they shall run upon the wall, they shall climb up upon the houses; they shall enter in at the windows like a thief. **10** The Earth shall quake before them; the heavens shall tremble: the sun and the moon shall be dark, and the stars shall withdraw their shining: **11** And the Lord shall utter his voice before his army: for his camp is very great: for he is strong that executeth his word: for the day of the Lord is great and very terrible; and who can abide it?

(This is at the end of the Millennium and it is where the church (believers in Christ) physically fight the army of the devil to defend Jerusalem and the whole Earth. This battle will range worldwide and it seems everything is consumed by the fire that proceeds us and follows us in this battle.)

Remembering Hebrews 10:31 'It is a fearful thing to fall into the hands of the living God.'

Lucifer-Satan's final end:

> Ezekiel 28: **18** Thou hast defiled thy sanctuaries by the multitude of thine iniquities, by the iniquity of thy traffick (what the Devil was promoting. Either products and or philosophy); therefore <u>will I bring forth a fire from the midst of thee, it shall devour thee, and I will bring thee to ashes upon the Earth</u> in the sight of all them that behold thee.

> **19** All they that know thee among the people shall be astonished at thee: thou shalt be a terror, and never shalt thou be any more.

> (Remember only God who created the angels can take their life away from them and this is how Lucifer-Satan will meet his end after the final war following the Millennium and the White Throne Judgment.)

Summary of what I hope you've learned in the above scriptures.

I have put together the scriptures relating to Lucifer in Heaven before he fell. He was beautiful, full of wisdom and perfect in all his ways. Then he was given the assignment as Covering Cherub for Earth. To accomplish this gigantic task he enlisted angels that he probably worked with during his time in Heaven. There were at least one third of all the angels and probably more. I say more because of the size of this task and that I don't believe all of the angels that went with him on this assignment would have followed him in his attempt to overthrow God.

It is not known or indicated in scripture how long it took for Lucifer to become indifferent towards God, but we know it happened. Keep in mind that even today when some in the Church get power and wealth God seems to become distant to them and not by His choice. They become self-reliant, and sometimes self-absorbed, but always they have less time for God and don't feel they need to pray for anything. Also the temptations just slowly begin to draw them in deeper and deeper. Scripture does tell us that Lucifer had experienced this as his accomplishments piled up along with his wealth and pride in his beauty. He had free rein as he ruthlessly ruled over the nations in anger. It seems he was probably given reprimands. I'm also sure he would have resented them and ignored them.

Now I know God knows all things past, present and future, so as to why He put Lucifer in charge of the Earth back then knowing he would eventually rebel is a little beyond me. However, when you give it some thought, as I have, there is an answer and that is that God wanted to give His created race of spirit beings, the angels, the opportunity to make a free will choice to follow Him willingly. Because up to that point they really hadn't had an opportunity to make that choice for themselves. There was never any danger that Lucifer would defeat God. I don't feel, from the evidence we have, that the angels really understood how powerful God actually is.

And here is my reasoning, through inspiration from God I believe, for this conclusion. Lucifer, Satan's name before he rebelled against God, was created by God and he was an angel of high rank. In fact, he was a Cherubim and because of his service in Heaven for an undetermined period of time God placed him as the Covering Cherub over planet Earth as it was back then. In order to bring Earth and its population to a point where it would become a functioning independent civilization, which knew about God and also worshiped Him. To accomplish this task for God Lucifer recruited his friends and cronies that he had worked with over the time that he was on different assignments for God in Heaven.

Now, we understand from scripture that this amounted to at least one third of the angel population of that time and maybe even more. And at that point when he accepted this assignment Lucifer was blameless in his behavior from the day he was created until wickedness was discovered in him. Probably many thousands of years into his reign here on Earth. And from Ezekiel 28:15 we know that during his time in Heaven, before he was placed as the anointed covering Cherub over Earth he was upon the holy mountain of God. He had walked up and down in the midst of the stones of fire. But he would have been consumed by holy fire if he had sin in him then. It is even a fair speculation that Lucifer may have led worship sessions seeing that he had actual musical instruments embedded in his body. But we have to balance this understanding with scripture which tells us that sin cannot live in close proximity to God the Father therefore for Lucifer to have walked between the stones of fire on God's holy mountain Lucifer had to be sin free at that point in his life.

Therefore knowing Lucifer would lead a rebellion against Him and one third of the angels would follow him in that rebellion, God only taught the angels the lower secrets of Heaven. In other words, they were selectively educated. We know this from The Book of Enoch. Remember scripture tells us that Lucifer was full of wisdom and perfect in his ways at this point. So, he and the other angels were not stupid beings. Therefore, and I believe it through inspiration, God only presented Himself to them as the ruling monarch who was a being similar to them. Much like we experience the Royal Families of this world today.

We know from Job that the angels witnessed God place the Earth's cornerstone and lay its foundation so it is a mystery to me how they would ever believe they could defeat Him. They had seen God's full power in action. They should have trembled in awe before Him, but they believed they had the power, might and wisdom to overthrow Him as King. The only thing I can think of for their very flawed reasoning is that they became delusional and arrogant from their successes and the wealth they had all accumulated while on Earth. There is no way of telling how long this took.

In God's eyes they all had to be given the chance to choose as to whether or not to follow Him willingly or follow Lucifer and try to overthrow Him. God knew this was coming in the future. However this is the same choice God allowed Adam and Eve, out of their free will, to make. Obey Satan or obey God. Unfortunately, as we know now, they chose to obey Satan and for this Adam lost control of the Earth back to the Lordship of Satan. This is the same choice all of mankind has been given since then. Obey God or obey Satan. Jesus was given the same temptation while he fasted in the wilderness Matthew 4:1-11; Luke 4:1-13.

Look at Satan's track record since he chose to rebel:

1. He openly disobeyed God when setting up his earthly civilization before Adam.

2. It took Lucifer several thousand years to build a civilization that only knew how to sin Jeremiah 4:22

3. Lucifer rebelled and tried to overthrow God as ruler of this Universe. Ezekiel 28; Isaiah 14

4. He lost his rebellion and the civilization he created was destroyed utterly. Jeremiah 4:23-28 This was the first flood.

5. Satan stole rulership of the Earth back from Adam Genesis 3:1-24

6. Once he had the Earth again it was party time all over again. It only took him and his angels 1650 years (time since Adam's fall) to again create a civilization from which God could only find one righteous man and his family, Noah. This was the second flood Genesis 6:9 - 8:22

7. Since Noah's flood Satan has basically gone underground. He stays in the shadows as much as possible and has his human minions stay in the limelight. Oh he pops up every now and then but for the most part he pushes his agenda from the shadows of his dimension.

The angels are created spirit beings from the beginning. They saw the power of God at work (Job 38:7) and yet they still tried to overthrow Him and put Lucifer in His place on the throne. When they consciously, with their free will, chose to do this there was no turning back for them. Their fate was sealed for eternity. However, when God made man in His image, a three part being, He had also made provisions for man's forgiveness (Revelation 13:8). Remember that we discussed earlier how this was decided and implemented after Lucifer's world had been overthrown. This was also the same time the Lamb's Book of Life was implemented.

When a person accepts Jesus into their life, the following occurs and this is the process for that change to our eternal spirit:

John 3:**3** Jesus answered and said unto him, Verily, verily, I say unto thee, Except a man be born again, he cannot see the kingdom of God. **5** Jesus answered, Verily, verily, I say unto thee, Except a man be born of water (human birth) and of the Spirit (rebirth through faith in Jesus), he cannot enter into the kingdom of God.

Romans 10:9 That if thou shalt confess with thy mouth the Lord Jesus, and shalt believe in thine heart that God hath raised him from the dead, thou shalt be saved.

2 Corinthians 5:17 Therefore if any man be in Christ, he is a **new creature: old things are passed away; behold,**

all things are become new. (A new spirit being is created within us and that is our rebirth)

CHAPTER 3

Were There Two Floods?

We've looked at the scriptures which told us about Lucifer and his reign here on Earth as the Covering Cherub. So now, we'll look at the scriptures and make a comparison between what I'll call Lucifer's Flood and Noah's Flood. Let's see if there are any stand out differences or could these scriptures be talking about the same event?

Lucifer's Flood

1. Earth made waste & empty of life (Gen 1:2, Jer 4:23)

2. Heavens made totally dark (Jer 4:23, 27-28; Gen 1:2-5)

3. Vegetation destroyed & then recreated (Jer 4:23-26; Gen 1:2-12)

4. Water taken off in one day. God rebuked the waters (Gen 1:6-12; Psalm 104:7)

5. At end of Satan's flood God set bounds for the water (Psalm 104:9)

Noah's Flood

1. Earth not made waste & not empty of life (Gen 8:11-12; 22; Gen 6:17-22; 8:16)

2. Light was not withheld from heavens (Gen 8:1-22)

3. Vegetation not destroyed (Gen 8:11-12; 22)

4. Natural abating of water (Gen 8:1-14)

5. At end of Noah's flood no bounds for water set (Gen 8:2)

<table>
<tr><td>

6. Because all light withheld from Earth all sea creatures died (Gen 1:2, 20-23; Jer 4:23-26)

</td><td>

6. No fish were destroyed (Gen 6:18-8:22)

</td></tr>
<tr><td>

7. No fowls, animals, fish nor man survived (Gen 1:20; 24-28; Jer 4:23,24)

</td><td>

7. Fowls, animals, men and women were on the Ark. No fish were harmed (Gen 6:18; 8:17)

</td></tr>
<tr><td>

8. There was no social system (2 Pet 3:6; Jer 4:23-26)

</td><td>

8. A social system was left (Gen 6:18; 8:22, 2 Pet 2:5)

</td></tr>
<tr><td>

9. No Ark to save anything (Jer 4:23-26; 2 Pet 3:6-8)

</td><td>

9. Ark built to save life (Gen 6:14-22; 1 Pet 3:20)

</td></tr>
<tr><td>

10. Cause was Satan's rebellion (Isa 14:12-14; Jer 4:23-26; Eze 28:11-17; Luk 10:18)

</td><td>

10. Cause was fallen angels; wickedness of men (Gen 6:1-13)

</td></tr>
</table>

Quite obviously, these scriptures are not speaking about the same event. Lucifer's flood, described in Jeremiah 4 resulted in a total extinction event, and describes the total destruction of cities and all life on Earth in a totally destructive deluge. Then, God Himself turned off all the lights of the Universe, and I would say that brought on a worldwide Ice Age, destroying all plant life and aquatic life as well. Now, the scriptures don't tell us how long the lights of the Universe remained off, but they do tell us that they were restored in the next stage of God's creation process described in Genesis. In this current stage of creation, God created man in His image when He breathed His spirit into him. In Noah's flood, men, women and animals were preserved on the Ark, and we know that vegetation was not destroyed totally because the dove brought back a freshly picked olive leaf in its mouth.

The comparison has shown that there were two distinct flood events described in the Bible, but is there any physical evidence from Archeology that backs this conclusion up? Well, as it so happens, there are two very large prehistoric bone beds of ancient animal skeletons. One is found in South Africa, and the bones are completely fossilized. To be clear, scientists have determined that it takes at least 10,000 years for bones to be fossilized, and in the South Africa bone bed they found all fossilized bones. However, at Hell Creek Formation in Montana and South Dakota, none of the dinosaur bones that were found are fossilized. We'll talk more about this later in this chapter.

Let's stay with the South African bone bed first. In the vicinity of Langbaan Western Cape, South Africa, there is a Fossil Park that contains the bones of over 200 different species of animals. It has been called an **animal salad** that contains bones of giant wild pigs, over 40 specimens of *aardvarks*, numerous long-necked and short necked giraffes (sivatheres), and 5 different species of hyena. It also held an extinct form of hippo, a three-toed horse called *hipparion*, 3 species of elephants, *bontebok* antelopes, as well as the *boselaphine* which today is found only in Asia, a saber-toothed cat, a wolverine, an enormous African bear, and a large number of smaller animals.

There are no less than 10,000 identified bird bones so far, representing 90 different species, including marine birds such as cormorants, penguins, and an albatross, shorebirds, songbirds, parrots, woodpeckers, and at least one species of ostrich. Of even more importance, included in the jumble of bones are those of seals, whales and megalodon sharks, creating a mixture of marine, avian, and land mammal bones that were laid down in this single catastrophic event. **(An article by Len de Beer, Creation Magazine 38(3) 2016)**

Just in case you missed it, they found 10,000 bird fossils so far. Quite a large list of modern day bird species were found fossilized mixed in with the dinosaur bones. No one is mentioning them or displaying any of these modern day bird fossils that were found along with the dinosaur fossils. No Museum is displaying these modern day bird fossils, and no one is mentioning the fact that no evolution has taken place in these bird species, yet they too lived with the dinosaurs. The reason no one is mentioning or displaying these modern day fossilized bird bones is because they prove there has been no evolution. That's right, there is no evidence of evolution in these bird species since the Age of the Dinosaurs. They don't fit into the accepted Dogma of Evolution. I find this hidden truth infuriating. To think that we trust these scientists, archeologists and museum curators to display the facts and tell us the truth about our past, when quite obviously they all haven't been doing that. They are quite obviously promoting evolution and hiding the truth from the public.

Dr. Carl Werner's book and DVD, **Living Fossils**, reveals that fossil researchers have found many modern bird remains with dinosaurs, yet museums do not display these fossils, thus keeping this information from the public. Dr. Werner visited 10 dinosaur digs and 60 museums all over the world. He interviewed various paleontologists during which he compiled a list of modern bird fossils found with dinosaur fossils.

Dr. Werner discovered that many types of modern bird fossils have been found with dinosaurs including ducks, loons, flamingos, albatross, owls, penguins, sandpipers, parrots, cormorants, avocets, as well as extinct birds such as Mononykus, Archaeopleryx and Hesperornis. While these extinct birds did have teeth, there were many other modern types of birds without teeth that have been found. *(So no evolution of these birds: By leaving this fact out, the museum displays mislead the public.)* **(Creation Magazine 34(3) 2012)**

Okay, now Dr. Werner confirms what has been suspected for decades: that museums, evolutionists, scientists, schools and government officials and agencies have been working together to systematically promote and teach the false narrative of evolution.

The other part of these conspirators is the News Media, and the total silence that is echoing from their supposed halls of truth. Although, there are still some Media publishers that are trying to get the truth out like *Creation Magazine* and other Christian websites, as well as YouTube. However, the mainstream Media's total silence on these glaring discrepancies should be a flashing neon warning sign to every scientist that says they believe in the truth, and to every Christian, because they are hiding in plain sight their efforts to conceal the proof that the Bible and your faith are real and can be proven.

Stand up and start fighting back, Christians, and also get rid of the evolution stumbling block to your witnessing programs. Add to this the fact that they have been looking for a missing link for humans or any animal since Darwin put forth this garbage theory in 1859. Their success rates for this endeavor is 100% ZERO. Also, keep in mind always that the evolutionists have a very tenuous relationship with the truth. This becomes very apparent in their rush to find the elusive missing link to man and animals. Since Darwin's publication in 1859, there have been many frauds put forward as proof of this missing link:

- Java man in the 1890s
- Ramapithecus Man in 1904
- Piltdown Man in 1912
- Nebraska Man in 1920
- Lucie in the 1930s

All of which have been proven to be fakes for the missing link.

However, these frauds are still seen in full-color renderings in school textbooks and displayed in museums around the world as facts that men evolved from apes. There have also been numerous fakes put forward for the missing links of evolution in the animal kingdom. All eventually proved to be fake, but no retractions have ever been given.

Winston Churchill said, 'A lie can travel halfway around the world before the truth has a chance to get its pants on.' I think that was right for Churchill's time, but today it only takes seconds for a lie to spread all the way around the world on social media platforms.

The Dating Game

Up until now, we have looked at many things that should cause you to ask questions of Evolutionists regarding the believability of their claims of rock-solid evidence for evolution. You should be wanting to question archeologists and scientists about the accuracy of the time periods they have established in past years, because they don't seem to be holding up as new evidence determined with these new technologies enhancing science and new discoveries, which brings into question old norms, and this is happening on both sides of this argument.

Remember that the evolutionists are maintaining belief in the hundreds of millions of years, as well as telling us that men of our modern variety have only been here for 10,000 years. The creationists are also wrong, claiming the Earth and man have only existed for a maximum of 6,000 years. Both are ignoring, or they are totally unaware, that the Bible teaches that Lucifer ruled this Earth for an unknown period of time… long before this current stage of creation started with Adam and Eve. **BOTH** positions are too rigid, with no room for new facts to be considered.

The evidence that I have seen from the Bible, science, geology, and archeology indicate that everyone should take a step back and just re-examine the evidence again with open minds and hearts. They have found many thousands of fully fossilized dinosaur bones around the world. This physical evidence is very hard to ignore, especially when the scientists have said it takes 10,000 years for a fossil to be formed. That places all the fossils far beyond the Creationist timeline of only 6,000 years old, by any reasonable argument. But, it does point to the Two Floods.

If you remember in the Jurassic Park scenario, the scientists found dinosaur blood in dinosaur mosquitos trapped in tree sap that had formed into amber. That was probably an impossible scenario, just as impossible as finding 65 million year old dinosaur bones that haven't fossilized yet and miraculously contain blood cells, DNA, bone cells, flexible tissue samples. If a screen writer or book author came up with this idea, they might not receive the best reception. That is just too farfetched to even consider. Then try and imagine how much I had to readjust my plausibility scale when I read the following article, because it sure looks like Jurassic Park is a very viable concept now. Here is why:

At Hell Creek Formation in Montana and South Dakota (so it is not a small area), hundreds of unfossilized dinosaur bones (some full skeletons) still smell like putrefied corpses when dug up. This sounds like they haven't been buried long enough to become fossilized. Remember, fossilization takes at least 10,000 years, according to science. Yet, the evolutionists ignore their noses and stubbornly claim these bones are millions of years old. I have learned in my life, as much as you would like too, you can't have it both ways. Scientists have found blood cells, flexible tissue in a Triceratops Horn, but they say they've been extinct for 65 million years. Flexible ligaments, protein, blood vessels, collagen, and not just one or two, but all of these finds should not, would not, exist if these bones had been buried for 65 to 200 million years.

Where's the apology, 'We were wrong', 'We have to relook at the evidence' or how about 'We're sorry for our false assumptions.'?

And again, we see here the impact that can be gained from the Media's total silence on this issue. The reality here is that only a small group of people know about this dynamic opinion changing information. Christians, what do you think your Evolutionist acquaintances would have to say about this information? "What do you think Science would reveal about this information if they investigated it with an open mind and from a Biblical perspective that there were two floods. One flood under Noah and the first flood under Lucifer many thousands of years ago?" Unfossilized remains probably would fall under Noah's flood given that it takes 10,000 years to form a fossil. Every fossilized remains of dinosaurs, and modern creatures still roaming and flying in the skies today would fall under Lucifer's flood, which was many thousands of years ago.

Here are the quietly published articles about these finds:

At the same Hell Creek, Montana, Dr. Mary Schweitzer discovered dinosaur blood cells. She said 'If you take a blood sample, and you stick it on a shelf, you have nothing recognizable in about one week. So why would there be anything left in dinosaurs?' Schweitzer recounts how she noticed that a T Rex skeleton (from Hell Creek, Montana) had a distinct cadaverous odor. When she mentioned this to long-time paleontologist Jack Horner, he said, 'Oh yeah, all Hell Creek bones smell.' But so ingrained is the notion among paleontologists that dinosaur bones, such as the Duckbilled dinosaur at Hell Creek, must be millions of years old therefore the smell of death didn't even register with them despite the evidence being right under their noses. They've also lost the ability to question!

There have been other unexplained things found at Hell Creek.

- In 1993, dinosaur bone blood cells give Dr. Mary Schweitzer 'goosebumps'.

- In 1997, hemoglobin, as well as recognizable red blood cells in T Rex bone.

- In 2003, evidence of the protein osteocalim was found.

- In 2005, flexible ligaments and blood vessels were found.

- In 2007, collagen (an important structural protein in bone) in T Rex bone.

- In 2009, the fragile proteins elastin and laminin, and further confirmation of collagen - in a duck-billed dinosaur (If the dinosaur fossils truly were as old as claimed, none of these proteins should have been present.)

- In 2012, bone cells (osleocytes), the proteins actin and tubulin, and (DNA) were reported. (Measured rates of decomposition of these proteins, and especially DNA, show that they could not have lasted for the presumed 65 million years since dinosaur extinction. This is more in line with the Biblical timeline of thousands of years, but I don't mean just 6,000 years.)

- Researchers at Hell Creek South Dakota studying the fossil remains of duckbill dinosaurs have found a vast array of dinosaur "blood cells, soft tissue" within the bones. This latest find includes bone cells, blood cells, blood vessels and fibrous collagen-like structures. They also made the first-ever discovery of osteocytes and blood vessels from a dinosaur backbone and its bony (ossified) tendons. Scientists examined 17 unfossilized (i.e. not per-mineralized) dinosaur bones of various types from a mass mortality bone bed (graveyard).

Every bone sample at Hell Creek contained *osteocytes* (the longest living bone cell scientists know of), described as abundant in 10 of them, and another 5 as frequent (I sincerely doubt they would live for millions of years). Sixteen of these 17 samples contained blood vessels, some of which were described as hollow and even slightly pliable upon manipulation. In addition, 14 of the bones were found to contain collagenous matrix. (The discovery of unfossilized dinosaur soft tissue is problematic for those who believe that dinosaurs died out millions of years ago. But the discovery, and the vast number buried together in similar graveyards, makes perfect sense when we understand that most such fossils (called fossils but not yet fossilized) were formed as a result of Noah's flood just a few thousand years ago. (**Creation Magazine 42(1) 2020**)

Ullmann, P., Pandya, S., Nellermoe, R., *Patterns of soft tissue and cellular preservation in relation to fossil bone tissue structure and overburden depth at the Standing Rock Hadrosaur Site, Maasrichtian Hell Creek Formation, South Dakota, USA, Cretaceous Research 99, 1-13, July 2019*

This also confirms that there were two floods. One at the end of Lucifer's rebellion which produced the fully fossilized dinosaur bones that have been found worldwide, and Noah's flood, which have produced mass grave sites such as these in South Dakota and in Montana, all in the Hell Creek Formation. Since Science tells us that it takes 10,000 years to form a fossil, we can say for a fact that this find proves there were two mass casualty events in the history of this world, and both by flood.

Evolutionists are just guessing at dates?

In 2012, radiocarbon discrepancy was reported. (But carbon-14 decays so quickly that if the remains were even 100,000 years old, none should be detectable). (**Double-decade dinosaur disquiet, David Catchpoole Creation Magazine 36(1) 2014**)

Radiocarbon dating has been shown to not be reliable in a sample of fossils containing sandstone, mussels and coalfield wood. (Now, remember it takes at least 10,000 years to form a fossil.) The sample was tested in Zurich Switzerland by conventional rock dating methods and with Radiocarbon dating for the coalfield wood. The sandstone was dated at 20 million years and the coalfield wood from the very same fossil sample was dated at 36,000 to 40,000 years. (This is a difference of a factor of around 500 times. Why? How can the same fossil contain an age variation of this size? Logic would dictate that we assume the date of the fossil to be of the lessor amount or this fossil formed and then unformed close to 20 million years later where it ran into the wood and then reformed as a fossil. That makes no sense at all.)

Dating in Conflict, Creation Magazine 19(2) March - May 1997

I want you to really think about how Evolutionists have been just guessing and estimating when things went out of existence and came into existence. Their Scientists said grass evolved 55 million years ago. However grass was discovered in fossilized dinosaur dung from a Titanosaur. The problem for the Evolutionists is that they said the Titanosaur dinosaurs lived 145 to 66 million years ago. Now, that would mean the Titanosaur sauropod dinosaur ate the grass 11 million years before grass actually existed. In other words, as we said, these Evolutionists are just guessing at the age estimates. **Creation Magazine 29(4) Sept - Nov 2007**

The Sand Dunes in the Namib Desert in Southwestern Africa are among the world's largest, and possibly the most famous. They are routinely claimed to be the world's oldest, with quoted ages of 20 - 80 million years. But in a recent study in Geology, three scientists from the University of London concluded the dunes are only 5,700 years old at most. In fact most of the dune they studied, according to their calculations, is less than 2410 years old. (So, once again here is another problem with the Evolutionists age estimates) **Creation Magazine 29(4) Sept - Nov 2007; Geology 36(6): 555-558, June 2007**

Paleontologists have discovered a fossilized 25 ft. mysticete (baleen) whale well above sea level in the Santa Cruz Mountains of California. They say the well-preserved animals died around 4 million years ago. The evidence suggests a catastrophic, watery, event suddenly buried the Santa Cruz whale in sediment. **Creation Magazine 38(2) 2016**. (The evidence also suggest that since this animal is fully fossilized that this animal died in the catastrophic flood under Lucifer not Noah).

I feel that this new information proves there were two separate floods. One at the end of Lucifer's reign on Earth and the other in Noah's day

4360 years ago. Remember it takes 10,000 years to form a fossil and all the bones in the South Africa bone bed are fossilized, but the dinosaur bones in the Hell Creek bone bed are not fossilized yet. It proves the two flood theory, the GAP Theory and proves God created the dinosaurs. The sad thing about this is that most of the experts are treating the evidence as only one flood. This new data on Hell Creek and the Dinosaur bones found unfossilized seems to be being ignored.

Other examples here

The question that arises here is this. "Are there scriptures telling us that God created the Dinosaurs?" Let's look.

Job 40:15-24

15 Behold now behemoth, which I made with thee; he eateth grass as an ox. 16 Lo now, his strength is in his loins, and his force is in the navel of his belly. 17 He moveth his tail like a cedar: the sinews of his stones are wrapped together. 18 His bones are as strong pieces of brass; his bones are like bars of iron. 19 He is the chief of the ways of God: he that made him can make his sword to approach unto him. 20 Surely the mountains bring him forth food, where all the beasts of the field play. 21 He lieth under the shady trees, in the covert of the reed, and fens. 22 The shady trees cover him with their shadow; the willows of the brook compass him about. 23 Behold, he drinketh up a river, and hasteth not: he trusteth that he can draw up Jordan into his mouth. 24 He taketh it with his eyes: his nose pierceth through snares.

This sounds like a description of a large herbivore dinosaur. Possibly one of the following: the Dreadnoughtus which was 89 feet from head to tail, or the Patagotitan whose thigh bone is 8 foot end to end and its length was 122 feet with a weight of approximately 77 tons, or the Argentinosaurus 121 to 131 feet in length and approximately weighed 110 tons. There are many other large dinosaurs having tails that could be seen as large cedars. Early Bible scholars thought that the Behemoth was a Hippopotamus, but that was based on a guess with the limited knowledge of their time. Today a simple Google search for a photo of the Hippopotamus will show you its tail is totally inadequate for God's description of the beast. For anyone to say the Behemoth described by God to Job could not be one of these is certainly pushing the bounds of credibility.

Job 41

1 Canst thou draw out leviathan with a hook? or his tongue with a cord which thou lettest down? 2 Canst thou put an hook into his nose? or bore his jaw through with a thorn? 3 Will he make many supplications unto thee? will he speak soft words unto thee? 4 Will he make a covenant with thee? wilt thou take him for a servant for

ever? 5 Wilt thou play with him as with a bird? or wilt thou bind him for thy maidens? 6 Shall the companions make a banquet of him? shall they part him among the merchants? 7 Canst thou fill his skin with barbed irons? or his head with fish spears? 8 Lay thine hand upon him, remember the battle, do no more. 9 Behold, the hope of him is in vain: shall not one be cast down even at the sight of him? 10 None is so fierce that dare stir him up: who then is able to stand before me?

11 Who hath prevented me, that I should repay him? whatsoever is under the whole heaven is mine. 12 I will not conceal his parts, nor his power, nor his comely proportion. 13 Who can discover the face of his garment? or who can come to him with his double bridle? 14 Who can open the doors of his face? his teeth are terrible round about. 15 His scales are his pride, shut up together as with a close seal. 16 One is so near to another, that no air can come between them. 17 They are joined one to another, they stick together, that they cannot be sundered. 18 By his neesings a light doth shine, and his eyes are like the eyelids of the morning. 19 Out of his mouth go burning lamps, and sparks of fire leap out. 20 Out of his nostrils goeth smoke, as out of a seething pot or caldron. 21 His breath kindleth coals, and a flame goeth out of his mouth. 22 In his neck remaineth strength, and sorrow is turned into joy before him. 23 The flakes of his flesh are joined together: they are firm in themselves; they cannot be moved. 24 His heart is as firm as a stone; yea, as hard as a piece of the nether millstone.

25 When he raiseth up himself, the mighty are afraid: by reason of breakings they purify themselves. 26 The sword of him that layeth at him cannot hold: the spear, the dart, nor the habergeon. 27 He esteemeth iron as straw, and brass as rotten wood. 28 The arrow cannot make him flee: slingstones are turned with him into stubble. 29 Darts are counted as stubble: he laugheth at the shaking of a spear. 30 Sharp stones are under him: he spreadeth sharp pointed things upon the mire. 31 He maketh the deep to boil like a pot: he maketh the sea like a pot of ointment. 32 He maketh a path to shine after him; one

would think the deep to be hoary. 33 Upon Earth there is not his like, who is made without fear. 34 He beholdeth all high things: he is a king over all the children of pride.

Wow, now if that isn't describing a dragon, I would be flabbergasted.

Did you notice that in both these descriptions of dinosaurs, men were trying to capture or kill them, but having little success? Did you notice that men were mentioned by God in both of these animal descriptions and they were trying to capture or kill the animals described? Conclusion is that men walked with the dinosaurs. Next is a scriptural reference about the city of New Jerusalem that He is building in Heaven. I have included this passage to show the size of the pearls He is using for the 12 gates in the wall of this city. They are each so large, some 300 feet in diameter that only a dinosaur oyster could have produced them.

Revelation 21

1 And I saw a new heaven and a new Earth: for the first heaven and the first Earth were passed away; and there was no more sea. 2 And I John saw the holy city, new Jerusalem, coming down from God out of heaven, prepared as a bride adorned for her husband. 3 And I heard a great voice out of heaven saying, Behold, the tabernacle of God is with men, and he will dwell with them, and they shall be his people, and God himself shall be with them, and be their God. 4 And God shall wipe away all tears from their eyes; and there shall be no more death, neither sorrow, nor crying, neither shall there be any more pain: for the former things are passed away. 5

And he that sat upon the throne said, Behold, I make all things new. And he said unto me, Write: for these words are true and faithful.

6 And he said unto me, It is done. I am Alpha and Omega, the beginning and the end. I will give unto him that is athirst of the fountain of the water of life freely. 7 He that overcometh shall inherit all things; and I will be his God, and he shall be my son. 8 But the fearful, and unbelieving, and the abominable, and murderers, and whoremongers, and sorcerers, and idolaters, and all liars, shall have their part in the lake which burneth with fire and brimstone: which is the second death. 9 And there came unto me one of the seven angels which had the seven vials full of the seven last plagues, and talked with me, saying, Come hither, I will shew thee the bride, the Lamb's wife. 10 And he carried me away in the spirit to a great and high mountain, and shewed me that great city, the holy Jerusalem, descending out of heaven from God,

11 Having the glory of God: and her light was like unto a stone most precious, even like a jasper stone, clear as crystal; 12 And had a wall great and high, and had twelve gates, and at the gates twelve angels, and names written thereon, which are the names of the twelve tribes of the children of Israel: 13 On the east three gates; on the north three gates; on the south three gates; and on the west three gates. 14 And the wall of the city had twelve foundations, and in them the names of the twelve apostles of the Lamb. 15 And he that talked with me had a golden reed to measure the city, and the gates thereof, and the wall thereof. 16 And the city lieth foursquare, and the length is as large as the breadth: and he measured the city with the reed, twelve thousand furlongs.

[The length and the breadth and the height of it are equal. In modern measurement this is 1500 miles square and 1500 miles high with a corresponding size base for balance of this floating city of New Jerusalem.]

17 And he measured the wall thereof, an hundred and forty and four cubits, according to the measure of a man, that is, of the angel. 18 And the building of the wall of

it was of jasper: and the city was pure gold, like unto clear glass. 19 And the foundations of the wall of the city were garnished with all manner of precious stones. The first foundation was jasper; the second, sapphire; the third, a chalcedony; the fourth, an emerald; 20 The fifth, sardonyx; the sixth, sardius; the seventh, chrysolyte; the eighth, beryl; the ninth, a topaz; the tenth, a chrysoprasus; the eleventh, a jacinth; the twelfth, an amethyst. 21 And the twelve gates were twelve pearls: every single gate was of one pearl: [So let's make sure that registered in your mind. These Jasper walls surrounding the city are an impressive height and each of these 12 gates are carved out of one single pearl each. For a wall of this size and to allow a rider on a horse to pass through and also be structurally sound these pearls would have had to be at least 300 feet in diameter. Wow, let that sink in, now try to imagine the size of the oyster that produced each of them. Talk about dinosaur size animals and for sure God has them.] and the street of the city was pure gold, as it were transparent glass.

So the conclusion for the question "Did God create the dinosaurs?" is a resounding yes, and as we saw from the evidence at Hell Creek, Montana, God created them before Adam and again with Adam. The South African bone bed contains fully fossilized bone and the bone bed at Hell Creek is comprised of unfossilized dinosaur bones with a rotting cadaver stench. Remember, it takes 10,000 years to form a fossil, therefore, Hell Creek dinosaur remains haven't been buried for 10,000 years. I would say they were buried in the cataclysm of Noah's flood some 4300 years ago and the South African bone bed of fully formed fossils was buried in the cataclysmic flood after Lucifer's rebellion many thousands of years before Adam.

It is astounding to me that the same species of dinosaurs are found in both bone beds. They've found T-Rex, Duckbilled, Triceratops and many other dinosaur species in both sites. But remember, the South African site bones are completely fossilized and the Hell Creek, Montana bones are not fossilized.

To me this shouts

1. No Evolution! These species of dinosaurs found in both bone beds had not evolved

2. God created dinosaurs before Adam and with Adam

3. The elapsed time estimates are totally wrong

4. There were two cataclysmic floods thousands of years apart

5. The Elite scientists tell us that these species of dinosaurs lived 200 to 65 million years ago. But they don't offer us any explanation as to how it is possible for them to be finding blood cells, DNA, cologne, flexible blood vessels and ligaments in dinosaur remains at Hell Creek. If, as the experts say, these have been buried for at least 65 million years?

The simple answer is they don't know why and since this evidence (no Evolution, viable blood samples, flexible tissue) doesn't fit their accepted Dogma of Evolution they aren't commenting on it. However, these glaring facts still exist. They don't make these facts go away simply by not talking about them. It seems to me that the Bible is telling the truth. Lucifer reigned here on Earth and he created nations, cities and a civilization before he rebelled against God. The whole Earth was destroyed then (not the planet itself) and that damage was renovated in the Genesis account.

Summary Page One

Let's review some of what we learned in the last two chapters.

1. That the Bible tells us about Lucifer reigning here on Earth. Ezekiel 28:2-18

2. That Lucifer was assigned the position of Covering Angel over Earth by God. Ezekiel 28:14

3. That Lucifer was in Heaven before this assignment. Ezekiel 28

4. That Lucifer was Satan's name before he rebelled and lost.

5. Lucifer and at least 1/3 of the angels came to Earth and developed a civilization with cities and nations all around the Earth.

6. Yes there were men living on Earth before Adam. Jeremiah 4:25

7. Lucifer was full of wisdom and perfect in all his ways when he started this assignment for God. Ezekiel 28:12

8. Over a period of time Lucifer became rich, powerful, full of pride, and ruled with anger.

9. Lucifer led a rebellion with 1/3 of the angels to overthrow God as king and they lost.

10. The Earth's population at that time supported Lucifer in his rebellion.

11. God was so angry He destroyed every city Lucifer had built worldwide. Jeremiah 4:23-28

12. God flooded the entire world to destroy Lucifer's abominable creation.

13. Then God turned the lights of the Universe off to accomplish total destruction. Jeremiah 4:28

14. We compared the scriptures for the two floods, Lucifer's and Noah's, and found they were totally different and not the same event.

15. Also we saw there were dinosaur bones in two mass casualty events. One in Hell Creek Montana and the other in South Africa.

16. All the bones in South Africa were fossilized. None of the bones in Hell Creek were fossilized.

17. Remember it takes 10,000 years to form a fossil and Noah's flood occurred roughly 4350 years ago. Not enough time has passed for those bones to fossilize. Therefore, there were two separate floods many thousands of years apart.

CHAPTER 4

Something strange happened here on Earth long, long ago...

We use to have a saying, "It is written in stone." This meant that the information we were speaking about was irrefutable and to a degree we still follow this thinking today. However today if what has been found written in stone does not fit into an accepted timeline or dogma these facts are ignored or hidden from consideration. The internet offers a mix of truths, semi truths and outright lies which are thrown into a pot luck stew of information. This information is readily consumed by our young people as undeniable truths. But is there ever a thought given by them about researching to prove these so called facts for themselves? It seems the idea of truly fact checking has gone the way of the dinosaurs.

Photos taken in the Amazon in 1890 by British explorer Alfred Isaac Middleton. These native dwellings certainly resemble our shuttle and what looks like a UFO. The question that pops to mind is where did these people see these objects before they copied them?

That is a shame. Our education system use to teach the young people to question everything and not form an opinion until they had proven it for themselves. It is very concerning that this has become a lost art. If you accumulate enough proven information you are able to recognize subtle indicators in the new information you are consuming that cause your common sense to shout 'That Can't be Right'. School should be about teaching reading, writing, arithmetic, science and how to study information to come to our own conclusions. Elite Intellectual Professors tell us we evolved from apes. Is that true and backed up by evidence? Also that early humans were uneducated, unskilled hunter gathers before 20,000 years ago. But does the evidence support this?

And because it was our teachers and Professors who told us this we accepted its validity without questioning. Today people do the same thing with information that is presented on the internet. If we would just do some research in our own Libraries for example. I mean hardcopy books. If we did this we might find statements and evidence in those records that should raise your credibility sensors and ask 'how was this possible?' We definitely know humans didn't fly before the Wright Brothers in 1903 and there certainly was no space travel before the 1960s. But is that really true?

The pictures on the previous pages were taken of dwellings in the Amazon Rain Forest by British Explorer Alfred Isaac Middleton in the 1890s. How is it possible that one looks very much like our space shuttle and the other like a crashed UFO? Yet here is evidence that these dwellings existed in the 1890s. Before the Wright Brothers and definitely before NASA. Nobody today is asking these questions. Wouldn't you like to know why? I certainly would.

Now this very unusual Temple design in India has me again curious as to whether they could see into the future. Or this unusual Temple design is their attempt to honor their gods by replicating what they had seen. I do believe they were trying to duplicate what they actually saw these beings arrive in during an ancient encounter. What are your thoughts on this? These ancient people try to mimic in their construction what they saw in real life.

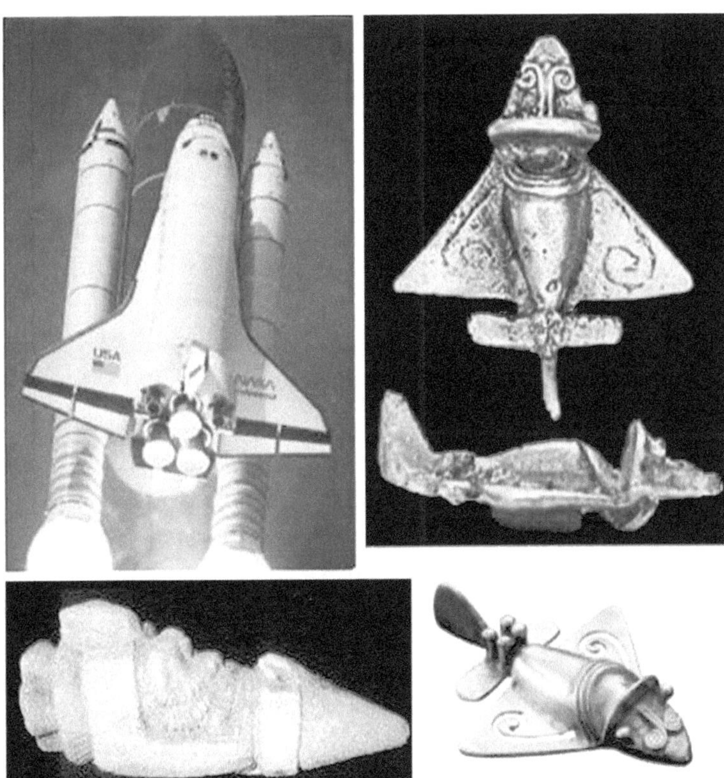

Here is a small golden artifact found in Columbia that looks very much like a Delta-wing aircraft. These objects suggest that earlier humans were exposed to mechanical flight technology and were simply copying what they had already seen in the sky.

The top picture is of a stone carving that is on display in the Istanbul Museum. It appears to be an astronaut in a space suite sitting inside a rocket ship or small shuttle craft covered in tubes. Below we also see a relief carving that was found in the Egyptian Temple of Seti 1 at Abydos. The wall relief carving clearly shows a Helicopter, an air craft, a satellite dish and what looks like a tank. There would be no way for them to just imagine these machines. The only conclusion is that they saw them here on Earth in our distant past. It doesn't seem like any of the so called experts are trying to determine what might have happened. But this book will give you the answers if you just keep reading.

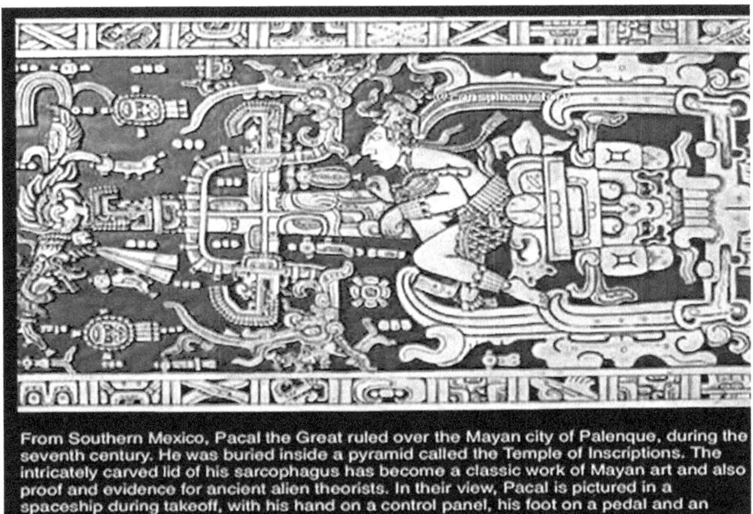

From Southern Mexico, Pacal the Great ruled over the Mayan city of Palenque, during the seventh century. He was buried inside a pyramid called the Temple of Inscriptions. The intricately carved lid of his sarcophagus has become a classic work of Mayan art and also proof and evidence for ancient alien theorists. In their view, Pacal is pictured in a spaceship during takeoff, with his hand on a control panel, his foot on a pedal and an oxygen tube in his mouth.

The above image is of the Aztec-carved stone coffin of Pacal the Great, who ruled over the Mayan culture. It sure looks like they were trying to mimic sending his body on a space adventure but where would they have even gotten this concept from unless they had seen this somewhere in their distant past?

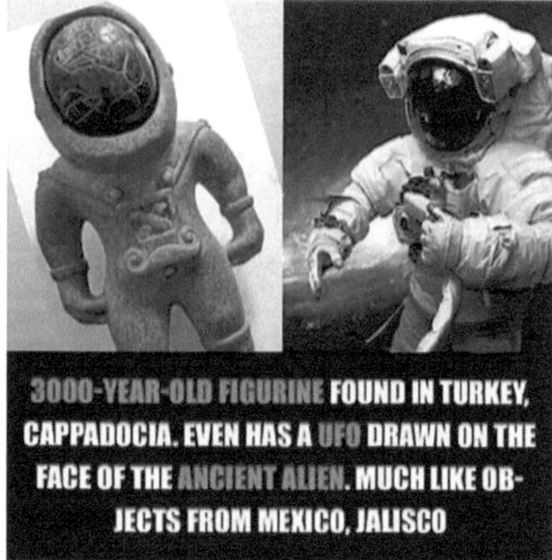

And here was see that somehow the culture in Turkey and the Mayan cultures many thousands of years ago were carving into stone examples of space suits. However we didn't design or use these until the 1960s. So these two cultures had visionaries that could see into the future and then had the skills to carve what they saw in stone? Highly doubtful, I'd say. Something happened here on Earth in the distant past that the Elite Intellectuals of the world today do not want to talk about nor form an opinion on these ancient pieces of evidence. Back then people carved only what they saw. No one would logically spend this amount of time and effort to carve something they imagined.

When you give it some thought these objects are really out of place in the timeline of history. Unless of course the timeline of history we have been taught is totally wrong. These images are examples of the ignored truths. The truth that humans, many thousands of years ago, came into contact with a race of beings that had very far advanced technology. But for some reason our Elite Intellectual Professors don't even want to speak of these oddities let alone research them for possible answers.

Then we find these carved images which resemble deep sea diving apparatus and astronaut helmet with communication microphones built into the helmet. These stone carvings took some time to produce so why would they spend so much time and energy on imagination to place in their respective Temples?

Here we see other versions of diving equipment which should not have existed in these ancient cultures but it apparently did and they made such an impression on the people that they reproduced them in stone figures as best as they could. Again these show something happened long ago in these ancient cultures where they came in contact with very advanced technology.

Strange Out of Place Knowledge Depicted

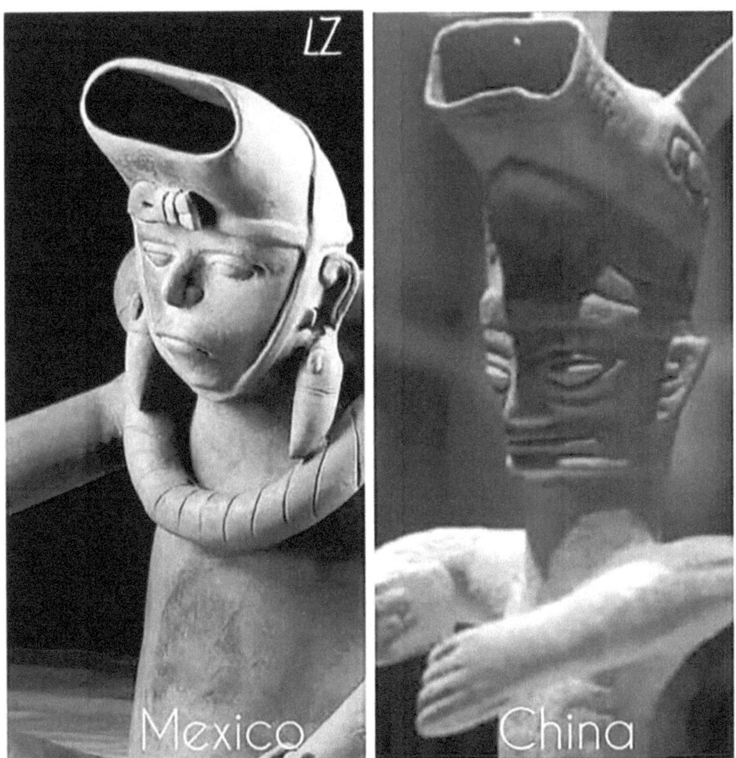

The Book of Enoch teaches us that the fallen angel AZAZ'EL taught the people the art of making swords, knives, shields and breastplates; and he also showed the women who were mating with the fallen angels how to make and use bracelets and ornamentation. He also taught them the art of makeup, shadowing of the eyes with antimony and the beautifying of the eyelids. Along with this he taught them about all kinds of precious stones and of all coloring tinctures and alchemy. Azaz'el taught all forms of oppression on the Earth.

I find it amazing that temple carvings from thousands of years ago depict confirmation that the fallen angels showed the daughters of men who they were sleeping with the art of makeup and fashion jewelry. These carvings are found in the Shirangam Temple, India.

The next question is did those fallen angels share advanced technology with the humans of that period? The previous examples of out of place technology and these stone carvings in the Gujarat's Palitana Temple seem to indicate YES. Looks like a cell phone and tablet to me with one of the girls using a stylist pen. I would say the fallen angels shared advanced technology with them what do you think?

The image below looks like a motorcycle to me. This was carved in several places. As you can see below 2 other people riding a bicycle carved on the wall of an Indian Temple confirmed by the IBTimes, which is published in India. Also found in two Asian Temples - one in Hampi, Karnataka and one in the Panchavarna Temple in Tamil, Nadu.

I'm not sure one can call this a mistake or imagination when the images of bicycle riding also appear in other different Temples around the world. But the Intellectual Elite try to tell us that it was someone's imagination, not a representation of real events. And in the case of the Indian temple bicycle carving it has been put forth that this carving was done during a 1990s renovation. This carving would have taken some time. So they would have us believe that they allowed the defacing of an ancient temple by some renovation contractor seemingly on a whim? And as I've stated the carving was confirmed as ancient by IBTimes in India. How stupid do they think the general public is?

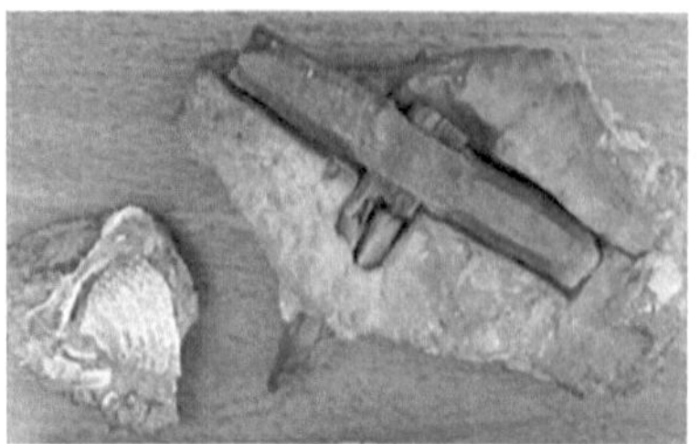

Out of Place Artifacts

Sledge Hammer 140 million yrs. old. **OUT OF PLACE**

In 1936 Texas a couple out for a walk found a Prehistoric hammer in the Travis Formation which is geologically 140 million yrs. old. The London hammer was imbedded in the stone formation and its wooden handle had already started the process of changing into coal. Modern Archeologists claim man has only been around 10,000 yrs. So they can't and won't even try to explain it. Thus it falls into the category of out of place artifacts. These artifacts do not fit into the mainstream chronology. A timeline that the Elites have set in place to promote their pet philosophies like evolution.

Transylvania, Romania

An aluminum hinge that should not exist. **OUT OF PLACE**

Unexplained hunk of aluminum found in Transylvania Romania in 1974 when workers in a construction site found the bones of two Wooly Mammoths at a depth of 35 feet. Now the experts in Archeology say the Wooly Mammoth went extinct 40,000 yrs. ago. So finding this aluminum hinge at the same depth with 3 holes drilled in it is perplexing to say the least. There is no explanation as to how the aluminum got there unless it was left or placed there beside the Mammoth bones 40,000 yrs. ago. Now add the knowledge that our industrial society didn't learn how to melt aluminum until the middle of the 19th century. Because this can't be explained the Transylvanian Museum removed it from public view.

Antikythera Device - Greece should not exist. **OUT OF PLACE**

Aegean Sea - April 1900 off the small Greek island of Antikythera they found an artifact that dated to the 2nd century BC. This artifact sat in storage in the

Athens National Museum for 60 years. Until John Price, a physicist, took a better look at it and found the box contained the workings of a highly sophisticated mechanical devise. What they can tell from inscriptions on it and how they think the device worked is that it was a highly sophisticated mathematical machine for predicting where the stars, sun, and planets were all going to be on a specific date. The scientists studying this artifact created this replica of what this artifact might have looked like when in use. The mere fact that this was in use in the 2nd center BC for this type of calculation would be a marvel in itself. But to have constructed and assembled all the wheels, cogs and ratchets that seemingly were involved here is amazing. This was not thought up, manufactured nor constructed by the locals. The scientists who studied the Antikythera tell us that it would have been able to plot ship voyages and crop cycles as well as plot Astrology movements. This is why it is called the "Ancient Greek Computer". The American scientists involved in the study said this would be like finding a Jet plane in the Tomb of King Tut.

'Greece has it on display for the public to view but it certainly raises a lot of questions.' (Ancient Aliens Program) Did the fallen angels help the designer and builder of the Antikythera devise? Remember the fallen angel BARAQIYAL taught astrology; KOKARER'EL taught the

Replica of the Antikythera Device

knowledge of the signs; TAMEL taught the seeing of the stars; and ASDER'EL taught the course of the moon as well as the deception of men. So with this added information would it surprise any of you that some fallen angel helped humans to build this advanced devise?

Think about this for a moment. It was found on a sunken ship in the Mediterranean, but the ship sank 3,000 yrs. ago. That means the inventors and makers of this machine would have had to know that the Earth was a sphere and that the planets revolved around the sun. They seem to have known precisely the cycles of the planets. They had to have known about the 235 lunar months for the calculations. Are we really to believe the people 3,400 years ago had the knowledge and the skills to produce the inner wheels, levers and cogs plus the skills of a watch maker to assemble it? They also would have had to understand the solar and lunar cycles along with the knowledge of the elliptical orbit of the moon. I don't know about you, but I find that a bit of a stretch in credibility.

To say the least these artifacts are totally out of place and time, but the Intellectual Elites don't even have a good guess as to where these artifacts came from or how they got to where they were found. They all seem to be impossibly out of place and time with no reasonable explanation for their existence. However they exist and that uniqueness puts them in front of the public. We must thank the media of earlier times because those reporters found these artifacts to be an extraordinary subject for a story and their publishers printed these stories. And it is because of this publicity that the public became aware of them which made them difficult to hide or cover up.

The fallen angels taught humans heavenly things.

Now let's get some things straight about the Book of Enoch (The Old Testament Pseudepigrapha 1983 The Book of Enoch). According to the Biblical timeline Enoch was translated (taken to Heaven without dying) 4 years before Noah was born. The book of Enoch was written around 200 B.C.E. So it's unlikely Enoch wrote this book himself and the author is unknown. That said, it has plausible information about the fallen angels and the advanced technology that was available to them. It give us some insight into angelic behavior before the Lucifer rebellion and after Adam's fall. The book shows the fallen angels activities and plans in a plausible way and from the results God had to later deal with we know the information was fairly portrayed. We are told that they revealed and taught the lower secrets of Heaven to men and every kind of sin. They then used women sexually, producing giants, which is what we see in Genesis 6. And the truth is that there was a rebellion and a war to overthrow God, which failed miserably.

Satan was already fallen when he tempted Eve in the Garden of Eden and The Book of Enoch states that these were fallen angels when Enoch (a descendant of Adam) met them. These fallen angels ask Enoch to take their petition for forgiveness to God. Now I look at that from a human perspective and ask 'Do humans in prisons ask for appeals to their cases?' and the answer is yes. So why wouldn't the fallen angels try for an appeal? It seems plausible to me and it was denied of course. Keep in mind these fallen angels knew God for a long time before they tried to overthrow Him. These same angels watch God set the cornerstone and the foundation of the Earth (Job 38:7).

Adam knew God, but had never seen Heaven nor walked on the Holy Mountain amongst the stones of fire which Lucifer had done and the other angels probably watched. So they knew God way better than Adam. Therefore no redemption was available to them. The Book of Enoch reminds us that these spirit beings do live right here on Earth and are actively working against humans. This is especially for Christians and Jews. The Book of Enoch also gives us insight into their past through its description of what they were doing when Enoch knew them. This in turn foreshadows what they may do in the future to humans. In our time today.

The Fallen Angel AMASRAS taught incantations and the cutting of roots and magical medicine; ARMAROS taught the resolving of incantations; BARAQIYAL taught astrology; KOKARER'EL taught the knowledge of the signs; TAMEL taught the seeing of the stars; ASDER'EL taught the course of the moon as well as the deception of men; AZAZ'EL taught the people the art of making swords, knives, and shields and breastplates; and he showed to their chosen ones (the fallen Angels' women) bracelets, decoration, shadowing of the eyes with antimony, ornamentation, the beautifying of the eyelids, all kinds of precious stones and of all coloring tinctures and alchemy. Azaz'el taught all forms of oppression on the Earth.

SEMYAZ - This angel was the leader of the fallen angels who mated with the women of the Earth and he led ARAKEB, RAME'EL, TAM'EL, DAN'EL, EZEQUEL, BARAQYAL, AS'EL, ARMAROS, BATAR'EL, ANAN'EL, ZAQE'EL, SASOMASPWE'EL, KESTAR'EL, TUR'EL, YAMAYOL, and ARAZYAL. These are the chiefs or lieutenants over tens and all those with them selected human women to have sex with. Their offspring were giants and men of renown.

We know these angels participated in these activities from Adam's fall through Noah. And their success (if you want to call it that) resulted in Noah's Flood (Genesis 8:11 - 12:22). Few realize that they probably did similar things and worse when Lucifer was the Covering Cherub over Earth. Which resulted in the First Flood that utterly destroyed the Earth (Jeremiah 4:23-28). Satan has a terrible track record in his dealings with humans in the past. Unfortunately his story didn't end there he just got better at hiding his plans. But Satan and his demons are actively warring against humans today whether or not we recognize it.

Now the problem in the past for figuring a historic timeline has been the lack of knowledge regarding a civilization ruled by Lucifer in the history of Earth. As you've seen in Chapter 3 there are scriptures detailing Lucifer's reign on Earth. Regrettably the Intellectual Elites have chosen to ignore those scriptures and by doing so they have become willingly ignorant. The knowledge from these scriptures also tells us that there was two different floods. Surely with just a little review of existing geological data it could be ascertained if there were two worldwide floods or not. Much to theirs and our detriment they are not even willing to entertain the thought of studying this new evidence from scripture.

Are the fallen angels still trying to lead humans astray?

In more modern days the angel MARONI interacted with a human Joseph Smith who started the Mormon Religion with what this fallen angel told him in the early 1800s. Maroni told Smith that he was from the star cluster Paladis. Now the Ancient Alien program says Maroni was an alien. However, if we follow the logic and evidence that Enoch laid out it is clear this is a fallen angel that finally found someone to listen to his lies. These lies have caused countless souls to miss the truth found only in Jesus.

The Voynich Code (according to a YouTube Video) should not exist. Now did the fallen angel AMASRAS taught the cutting of roots and magical medicine to the author of this mysterious book? Possibly. This is the world's most mysterious manuscript. Could this be a book on Root and Herbal medications, incantations, spells and astrological interpretations or predictions have been dictated to a human by a fallen angel such as Moroni did to Joseph Smith? Could it be written in the language of angels? Take some time to research the Voynich Code manuscript and see if it doesn't leave you scratching your head.

CHAPTER 5

Mega Construction

All over the world they are finding ancient ruins of construction that would be difficult, if not impossible, for modern man to duplicate today. This should raise questions like,

1. 'Why are they so incredibly well preserved?'

2. 'Who built them?' *(Fallen angels of Lucifer)*

3. 'Why and how were they destroyed?' *(Destroyed in First Flood after Lucifer's failed rebellion)*

4. 'Why has this level of construction knowledge been totally forgotten?' *(Everyone died in the first flood Jeremiah 4:23-28)*

5. 'How is that level of worldwide destruction even possible?' *(It was all destroyed by God Jeremiah 4:23-28)*

Think about it. The Intellectual Elites of the world (as Graham Hancock calls them) are not trying to answer these questions. They have no answer as to why that advanced construction knowledge was not past down to the next generation. Skills are

Gobekli-Tepe

always past down to the next generation. This has never happened before in recent history. But I've told you in chapters two and three who built them and you read it for yourselves from the Bible. This could only have happened with a mass extinction event. We know that we would struggle to duplicate these structures today. Yet the Intellectual Elites of Archeology and Science stubbornly hold to their timeline that even though hominids have existed on the Earth for 200,000 years, they were hunter gatherers and only started civilizations 8000 to 6000 years ago.

It also doesn't seem that these experts can even agree on dating these sites because **scientists can't date stone**. They have postulated that humans crawled out of caves some 10,000 years ago and suddenly began farming and developing communities, but they said they were not very intelligent and they used very primitive tools. That was considered as irrefutable knowledge and the timeline was not to be challenged until the discovery of Gobekli-Tepe in Turkey. It was accidentally discovered by a Turkish farmer and it covers an area of 20 acres or 48 hectares of land. It was discovered that this site was intentionally buried and that sand was tested and it was found to be at least 12,500 years old. This caused the Intellectual Elites to rethink their timeline because the news of Gobeli-Tepe had leaked out. Begrudgingly they set a new theoretical timeline and that's how the timeline got to 300,000 years of human existence. They arbitrarily added 100,000 years to their timeline. It's interesting to note here that even though the timeline was extended they still insist that the humans back then only had stone hammers and chisels to work with. The picture above of the Gobekli-Tepe site **certainly looks like they had better tools than that.**

One temple area contained over 500 cubic meters of soil and there are 20 temples in this site. Think of the organization it required for the construction of these temples. Contemplate about the vast amount of effort it took to quarry, transport, carve and erect the pillars in these 20 temples. It must have been very daunting. Especially considering the Intellectual Elites would have us believe it was done by a people barely out of caves. Even by today's standards using modern technology it would have been a massive undertaking. This type of structure certainly does not scream 'Built By Hunter Gathers' with stone hammers. What we see today is what's left after 11,600 years. This complex indicates a strong understanding of culture, farming and social interaction. A society that was developed far above the skill levels of Hunter Gathers.

Now if we take the dates already assigned by the Intellectual Elites for this site it is 7,000 years older than Stone Henge and 7,500 years older than the Pyramids. This is amazing in itself but they have recently discovered another site 46 kilometers east of Gobekli-Tepe and named it Karahan-Tepe. This new site covers an area of 4.2 acres or 10 hectares. I would say these discoveries confirm an ancient civilization that was developed far beyond the hunter gathers of the Intellectual Elite's timeline. This discovery made them look foolish. Gobekli Tepe is aligned to the Cygnus Constellation. It is said that Karahan Tepe is older than Gobekli Tepe by 1000 years and it is aligned to the Winter Solstice. The Archeologists say Gobekli Tepe was constructed near the end of the last Ice Age. According to the Intellectual Elites no wheel was invented yet and they could barely walk upright. So these misanthropes who were barely out of caves quarried the stone needed, carved all the pillars and used this site for 1,500 years. Then they intentionally buried the whole thing in sand and the whole human race promptly and collectively forgot who they were, how they built and carved it? Really?

Sacsayhuaman, Peru

Sacsayhuaman

Did the builders of the Sacsayhuaman complex use Geopolymers to create the stones or did they harvest the stone out of a massive lava flow? Now that is the question. First we have to explain what geopolymers are. This is the product of harvesting the limestone rock out of a quarry and then using a heat source of 900 to 1100 degrees Celsius to melt that natural limestone into a fluid form. During the melting process other types of stone can be added to increase the strength of the geopolymer that will be produced. Then it is a matter of transporting this liquid substance to the construction area. This would be much easier to transport than the carved rocks and the geopolymer could be poured to produce any size stone that was needed.

As you can plainly see the Sacsayhuaman site is huge and what you are looking at here are the three barrier walls which attackers would have had to breach before getting to the main complex.

You should notice that the stones in these fortress walls are of various sizes and bulge a bit in their middle. It is as if the weight of the rock above was causing the rock under its weight to bulge out. Hardened natural rock would not do that.

Notice the smooth surfaces, rounded corners and the stones that are bent to form the corner. I've never seen natural rock bend around corners though. Hammer and chisels don't usually leave such smooth surfaces and it would be almost impossible to accomplish such perfect joins that we can see on these stones. The archeologist say you can't even slide a razor blade between them. But all of these features could be achieved using Geopolymer stone.

Now these stone walls were deteriorating and it was going to affect tourism so the Peruvian Ministry of Culture in 2012 authorized a team of Peruvian, Russian and Ukrainian scientists to do a study on the rocks to determine why. This team was headed by Nikolai V. Berdnikov (PhD (Geol. & Miner.) The official report was issued in 2013 but not widely distributed and therefore not widely known. Also making distribution difficult is that the report is written only in Spanish and Russian. The report was called **'Plasticine Stones'** of Sacsayhuaman. The report was confirmed by the Far East Department of the Russian Mineralogical Society.

The Isida Project did a followup study and A. Kruzer produced a report of their findings.

It does seem a bit like someone is trying to hide the results of that study. They tested the composition of the Limestone rock in the quarry and from the wall itself. The limestone from the quarry was normal density with marbling and fossils throughout. The limestone from the wall more densely composed with no marbling or fossils present. The conclusion the scientists came to was that the limestone from the quarry was harvested, crushed to powder and then somehow liquefied and poured into place. They also found the larger lower stones of the wall had added material that was not limestone. This was thought to be for added strength to carry the weight of the wall above.

Sacsayhuaman, Peru

The studies also found that the limestone in the quarry had the perfect composition to produce Hydraulic Lime. But since Limestone from the quarry dissolved in a glass of vinegar it was assumed that a substance to harden the limestone against this was added to the mixture. Either that or the stones were coated with a protectant of some kind. However since the recent appearance of acid rain the stone of Sacsayhuaman may be eroding naturally now. The biggest mystery is who built Sacsayhuaman. The conventional answer is that the Inca built it in the 15th century. Alright, let's say they did. Why then did they not pass down these construction methods to the following generations? This type of construction is not evident anywhere but ancient ruin sites all over the world and especially not evident modern construction methods in South America. However there is another explanation that no one wants to consider or even talk about. Now the Intellectual Elites don't want to even consider this explanation because it comes from the Bible. That's right The Bible tells us that long before Adam and Eve Lucifer was sent to Earth to create a civilization as Covering Cherub *(Ezekiel 28:14)*, which included men (hominids) in nations and living in cities. Let's look at Puma Punku for more insight.

Puma Punku, Bolivia

A new study done by Joseph Davidovits, Luis Human and Ralph Davidovits is called the Ancient organic-mineral geopolymer in South American Monuments. Study done in 2018.

Puma Punku

As you can see, the site at Puma Punku is littered with very precisely cut stones and repeating patterns. Some of the stones are 7 meters high or 23 feet and weigh as much as 130 tons. Everything is precisely cut with right angles and sharp edges and the patterns that repeat are exactly the same. So precisely cut that there is no way they were done by hand with stone hammers and stone chisels. The H blocks are made of volcanic rock called Andesite. They are finely cut and they interlock with precision. Again an indicator that they were not hand cut. The faces of the H blocks are perfectly flat and their corners are exact right angles. All around the site you can find blocks with perfectly round holes and many with irregular holes in them. They were not cut with hand chisels. Nobody knows how old this site is but conventional archaeology tells us they were made around 536 AD with hand tools. No way.

Puma Punku

Researchers in 2018 used a scanning electron microscope on the H blocks and found organic matter, carbon and nitrogen inside the volcanic rock of the H blocks. Now having organic material inside volcanic rock is virtually impossible and points to the Andesite being a man made geopolymer. The sandstone blocks found at this site were also found to be geopolymers. The researchers then determined that the builders had mastered the art of making two different geopolymers. One for the Andesite used in the H blocks and one for the sandstone blocks. They now know that the builders of Puma Punku were far more advanced than the archaeologists are willing to admit.

The organic matter found in the Andesite stone of the H blocks is unheard of for volcanic rock therefore it indicates that it was made by artificial means. The SEM and petrographic evidence shows that these stones are far from being incredibly carved rocks. What we are looking at are two forms of ancient geopolymer concrete. This revelation at Puma Punku combined with what we learned from the study at Sacsayhuaman means there is now evidence of 3 different geopolymers having been used for construction in ancient times in South America. Apparently liquefied rock was not as rare as some would have us believe in the ancient world.

Peru

Egypt

Notice the little nobs sticking out of some of the geopolymer stone blocks in Peru and we can see them on blocks in the pyramids. Here we see the finely cut stones in the constructions found in Peru and in Egypt. Polymer material was found to be in the casing stones of the Pyramid. Perhaps more testing should happen in Egypt.

These walls are found at **Ollantaytambo, Peru** and just recently the stone was tested and it was found to be polygonal masonry or (in other words) a geopolymer (basically man made cement). According to; Lapshin R. Fabrication Methods of the Polygonal Masonry of large stone blocks with fitted curved surfaces in Megalithic Structures of Peru. Preprints 2021, 2021080087

Notice the little nobs sticking out of some of the geopolymer stone blocks in Peru and we can see them on blocks in the pyramids. Here we can see the finely cut stones in the constructions found in Peru and in Egypt. Polymer material was found to be in the casing stones of the Pyramid. Perhaps more testing should happen in Egypt

Cusco, Peru

Here the well-constructed foundation walls hold up the Catholic Church which was built on top of The Temple of the Sun. Notice the formed round corner of perfectly smooth stone bocks that in no imaginative way could have been cut by primitive tools.

Again the small knobs on the blocks, perfectly drilled holes, the sharp edges of the fitted stone blocks in the walls, perfect joints and smooth surfaces. We should all be screaming, 'Not done by hammer and chisel!' We should also understand these were produced by advanced technology. Technology and construction techniques that were far beyond the primitive Incas. The other thing we must remember is that the skills used to build these massive complexes were not past down to the next generation. The archeologists and scientists should be trying to determine why that is. Unfortunately they don't seem interested in determining that. They would rather impose a false timeline as to when these structures were built and their timeline is totally wrong. Stone or brass hammers and chisels were not used in the construction of these ancient structures.

Temple of the Sun

These structures were built thousands of years ago so how did they drill these holes? Not with hammers and chisels. Now they say the ancient Egyptians had a coring drill with a flywheel at top and a brass bit, but I've watched them demonstrated and they wobble a lot. As you can see the holes here are perfectly round and straight. Plus the stone block from Peru was not cut with hammer and chisel. There are no chisel marks, straight edges and smooth surfaces. It looks very much like it was formed in a mold with liquid geopolymer stone. Holes like these are found in many of the ancient ruins around the world, but there is just too much evidence available for me to fit it all in one book.

Found in the Temple of the Sun, Peru

These two drilled holes were found on the Pyramids in Egypt

Barabar Caves, India

Here you see the outside and inside of the **Barabar Caves in India** and there are 5 of these caves. The one pictured here was formed inside a massive piece of granite stone. No one is asking who produced these caves nor why nor when and especially not how did the ancients of India produce such finely finished work? As you can see it has been cored out and reminds me of the Toronto Subway Tunnels when they were drilling them underground. Notice the perfectly round arched ceiling with straight walls and flat floor. The walls and ceiling are all polished to a mirror finish. The Intellectual Elites would have us accept their story that this was done with hammers and chisels using torches as a light source. However there are no chisel marks and no evidence of soot from torches anywhere. You decide, 'Was it done by hand or ancient technology?'

Technology that was not past down to the following generations I might add again.

The walls of Baalbek, Lebanon

At Baalbek there is an ancient wall which has 6 megalithic stones in it 20 feet up from the ground. Now these stones weigh anywhere from 800 to 1100 tons and were quarried a little over 1/2 mile away. Then these stones were transported to the site and lifted up 20 feet and placed firmly into the wall structure. Now if you don't really give it much thought that may seem a reasonable feat especially with modern equipment. Well as it turns out there is a 7th sister stone to these left in the quarry and modern engineers tried to move it.

This seventh sister stone in the quarry is 64 feet by 19.6 feet by 18 feet and is estimated to weigh 1,650 tons. As it turned out **20 of our modern cranes** could barely lift it off the ground let alone move it 1/2 a mile and then lift it 20 feet up into place. Now if we can't do it today how in the world did the ancient people of that day, before the Greek and Romans, accomplish that very feat 6 times? Keep in mind the experts say these were quarried around 6,000 years ago. I say it is much older than that. The Intellectual Elites keep insisting that our ancient ancestors did just that. I agree only with ancient part of their statement. The ancient civilization who accomplished the quarrying and moving of these stones were from a now extinct group of hominids who lived under Lucifer's reign here on

Earth. However, they all died in the first catastrophic flood at the end of Lucifer's failed rebellion. (Jeremiah 4:23-28 KJV). The secrets of how they excavated and moved this size of stones died with them. The Bible is true folks whether you believe it or not.

Egypt

You are looking at the foundation stones of the Giza Pyramid. Just look at the size of these stones. They remind me of the Baalbek stones in Lebanon. Did you also see the little knobs on the very flat, perfectly formed stone just to the right of the two men? The little knobs remind me very much of the Geopolymer stones found in Peru. I wonder why they don't test for that here in Egypt.

This is the passage down to the basement of the pyramid so the foundation can be seen. This is very deep (as you can see) and is constructed out of massive stones comparable to the Baalbek Lebanon stones that we can't lift or move into place today. Now these foundation stones were supposedly quarried by hand with hammer and chisel 15

Egypt

kilometers down river from the Giza Plateau and then transported here. This was done supposedly 5,000 years ago. The above ground portion of the pyramid is constructed out of 590,712 stones ranging in weight from 2 to 70 tons. All quarried and moved by hand we are told with no modern equipment and the experts tell us this was all done in the life span of one Pharaoh. Now Herodotus, an early Greek historian and geographer, from around 450 BCE spoke of Temple Priests telling him about the Guardians of the Sky. These were beings that helped the ancient Egyptians by imparting knowledge and mechanized equipment to assist in doing this job quickly.

Now the Book of Enoch, (an extra Biblical text, useful for historical context) tells of God having very advanced technology, including flying machines. And The Book of Enoch tells us the angels were trained in Heaven and knew the lower secrets of Heaven, which they freely shared with the hominid population during Lucifer's reign on Earth before his rebellion and as well as after Adam's fall. (Ezekiel 28:4-18; Jeremiah 4:23-28; Isaiah 14:13-14 KJV) It should be noted that in both cases when the fallen angels openly shared knowledge with the humans of Earth the societies that existed fell into great sin both ended in a cataclysmic flood event brought on by God. (I compared both of these floods in chapter 3 of this book).

Here we have a relief carving from the **Temple of Seti at Abydos, Egypt**. In this relief carving we see a helicopter, satellite dish, a boat or a tank and a plane. I find this relief carving to be very supportive of the ancient stories of the off planet beings exposing the ancient peoples of Egypt to advanced technology. By off planet beings I mean fallen angels who are not from our planet or even our dimension according to the Bible. Even the most vivid of imaginations could not have depicted these vehicles without having seen them. Remember this was over 5,000 years ago. Add to this the fact that every ancient civilization on our planet have stories of sky beings coming down and interacting with the human population. Every ancient story ends in a cataclysmic flood. This would be referencing the first flood that destroyed Lucifer's world and all its cities and nations (Jeremiah 4:23-28 KJV). Now the Incas and Egyptians have ancient accounts that tell of the sky beings being able to float the stones from quarry to construction site. Now that sounds a little farfetched and I struggled with that until I ran across the fact that there exists such a stone enshrined in Japan.

Japan

This massive 500 ton behemoth of a rock has a recorded history of 2,000 years, but experts estimate it to be at least 16,000 years old. It floats 6 inches above the pool of water and has for over 2,000 years. They built a Temple around it in Takasago Japan. The Japanese say the gods descended from the heavens and used gigantic rocks to fly from place to place. Now look at this megalith stone and see how it has been precisely cut with channels and smooth surfaces. This stone was cut to fit into some structure. It was not formed this way naturally. Therefore I'd say that the ancient stories from around the world of sky beings, bird men or gods bringing

able to float huge stones into place now have valid evidence for their truth. This type of precise cuts and channels reminds me of the constructions in Peru.

However the mysteries in Japan don't end with the floating rock. They continue in **Asuka Park, Japan**. As you can see it is precisely carved with a smooth surface and two square holes that go all the way through. It was carved out of one solid piece of granite and weighs only a mere 800 tons. It has sat here where you see it for centuries and it serves no useful purpose at all. When it was carved and who carved it is totally unknown.

This underwater pyramid off the coast of Japan is not a natural formation. Notice the square cuts and edges. It is 165 feet long, 65 feet wide and 82 feet high. This is one solid piece of stone cut for a specific purpose and not an accident of nature.

The Intellectual Elites don't want to recognize this find in Japan and they have begun their disinformation campaign calling it a naturally created rock formation. Well it looks like man carved this rock to me. The Elites problem was that they started this false narrative before the whole area was examined. Look at the pictures below and see what was also found here.

These carvings were found at the Yonaguni Monument site on subsequent dives. I'll leave the decision up to the reader. Does this site now with this added information seem like it was a naturally created feature? This is more evidence that the Intellectual Elites of the world have their own agenda and timeline for creation and when something like this is found they try to explain it with totally ridiculous explanations. If that doesn't work they get the Media to ignore it by not reporting on it while the Elites pull all funding for study of the site. This structure was only in 1986 when our diving technology advanced enough for greater depths and longer periods of time underwater. However, till then no one knew anything about this megalithic structure. That means there were no records in history nor ancient stories that indicated it ever might have existed. The skill levels that were required to create this were not past down to the following generations. It was totally forgotten or the generation that created it were wiped out totally and their knowledge died with them. Lucifer's Civilization (Jeremiah 4:23-28 KJV)

Now before we move on to pyramids around the world I just found out about 24 huge man made caverns in Longyou County in China. They were found in 1992 by villagers in the village of Shiyan Beicun. According to local legends the many rocky pools of water in the area were bottomless. Some skeptical people decided to test this out by draining one and when they did they found the following.

There are from 24 to 36 of these caverns, which are not connected but separated by a 2 foot thick wall between each cavern. No one knows who carved these caverns out or when. Their origin has been lost to history. Or was this knowledge and skill lost in the first cataclysmic flood after Lucifer's failed rebellion? (Jeremiah 4:23-28 KJV) Just look at precision of the construction and the detail in the wall relief carving. The scale and complexity of construction involved here is mind boggling. Just look at the curvature on what looks to be a hallway. It has smooth walls and ceilings. This reminds me of the Barabar Caves in India. They definitely didn't construct these with hammer and chisel 2,000 years ago as has been speculated. We should keep in mind that the Chinese were meticulous record keepers even 2,000 years ago and an undertaking of this immense scale would have been recorded.

Egypt

This is a picture of the **Benben Pyramid** which was found in Egypt of course. Its properties were tested and it was found that not all of elements are found on Earth. This black ironstone is only found in meteorites. The mystery here is how the ancients worked with it and shaped it into its current form. This black ironstone is not difficult to break and for that reason for the ancients to use hammer and chisels to work it would be extremely difficult. And considering the accuracy of the angles and deviations it would have made it impossible for the ancients to work with this material without advanced technology. Another question is how they achieved such a high precision of polish. The level of polish on this stone reminds me of the **Barabar Caves in India** and the **Longyou Caves in China**. The question again arises, 'How in the world were the ancients able to produce these levels of polished finishes back then?' To add to these mysteries look at the delicate carving on the surface of this pyramid. Scientists who studied this work of art determined that it would be impossible for any tool, old or modern, to carve these inscriptions on this meteorite material. They concluded that it could only be accomplished with laser cutting technology. So how was this done thousands upon thousands of years ago? Bear in mind also that the caves were cut and polished in extraordinarily difficult materials and locations without modern lighting.

Precise knowledge of the Stars

The ancients had precise knowledge of the stars and aligned their structures to them. They are not only in Egypt. There are pyramids all over the world and very few people are talking about this fact. You see no one knows how the ancients on three different continents built similar structures in the form of pyramids. But they did and here's proof. The Xian Pyramids in China, the Teotihuacan Pyramids in Mexico and the Giza Pyramids in Egypt all align with the Constellation of Orion's Belt. Three different cultures located thousands of miles apart creating the exact same thing?

When I was in school back in the 50s and 60s we were only taught about the Pyramids in Egypt as if they were the only ones on Earth, but that was incorrect. As it turns out there are pyramids all over the Earth. There are pyramids in Bosnia in which they found organic material that tested to an age of 34,000 years ago. Much older than the pyramids in Egypt. An Archeologist named Osanagic discovered them but his study of them has been impeded by Egyptian Archeologist Zahi Hawass who has constantly worked against funding the Bosnian Pyramid excavation and study. Hawass' motivation looks like he wants to protect the accepted timeline of around 8,000 years and the Bosnian test results blow that right out of the water at 34,000 years.

The pyramids in the Kola Peninsula of Russian were discovered pre WW2 confirming the existence of an ancient civilization there. The Kola Peninsula pyramids are believed to be twice as old as the Egyptian pyramids which was confirmed when excavation was resumed last year. So what does this all mean? Well the evidence I've put forth in this chapter proves that an ancient and very advanced civilization existed worldwide at one time in the very distant past. No one knows who they were nor where they came from. There is only one concrete and documented account of that time period. That is from the Bible.

CHAPTER 6

Proof of Intelligent Design in the Stars

Okay, here goes my attempt to explain what God created in the heavens before He created the angels. God designed the constellations to pictorially tell the Messiah's story to the world. Think about that for a minute. He laid out His entire plan of redemption in the constellations before He created the angels or Adam. We know that the constellations existed before Adam because many of the examples of mega construction were lined up with the stars. Here are three examples.

1. The Toothuacan Pyramids in Mexico

2. The Great Pyramids in Egypt

3. The Xian Pyramids in China

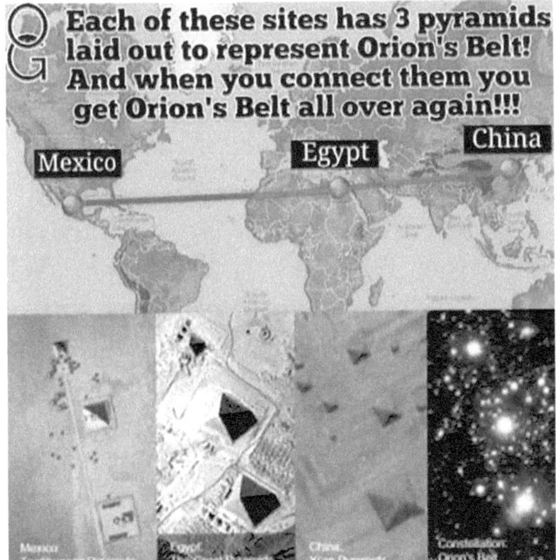

They are all aligned to Orion's Belt and the constellation depicts a male figure holding a club and shield. When I say lined up I don't mean roughly lined up I mean the pyramids at these three different sites around the world are exactly lined up with the stars of Orion's Belt.

The ancients called Orion's belt the Light of Heaven. So when Jesus said He was the Light of the World He was tying Himself back to the Constellation's story. Please remember that light pollution from our modern cities did not exist until the last 100 years. This light pollution effectively blocks us from seeing the constellations with our naked eyes. We live on Planet Earth, which is in a 9 planet solar system around a sun. Now this solar system is located inside the Milky-Way galaxy, which is one of many galaxies in the Universe that God created. The closest star to Earth is called Proxima Centauri, only a mere 4.22 light years away. Now with our current rocket speed it would only take us 137,000 years to get there.

Wow, that sure sounds like a doable trip. Not! NASA estimates there are over one trillion galaxies in the Universe. To me that means this was no small feat of creation on God's part. The closest galaxy to ours is called Andromeda and it's a mere 2.5 million light years from Earth. If we could travel at the speed of light, which we can't, it would only take 2.5 million years to get there and the Bible tells us that God can measure this entire Universe with the span of His hand. So it can be said that God and His capabilities are far beyond anything we could imagine.

Add to this the fact that God named each and every star and calls them all by name. I can barely remember what my wife sends me to the basement for. This is mind boggling to me. Today we have the Hubble Telescope orbiting the Earth and that is giving us a much larger view of the Universe. We have had an explosion of knowledge in the last 100 years and that has brought us super computers that can perform many tasks in seconds that use to take us days to figure out. Now I find it amazing that God predicted this increase in knowledge almost 2600 years ago through the Prophet Daniel.

> Daniel 12:4 But thou, O Daniel, shut up the words, and
> seal the book, even to the time of the end: many shall run
> to and fro, and knowledge shall be increased.

Almost two thousand years ago Jesus' disciple John (while a Roman prisoner on the Isle of Patmos) wrote The Book of Revelation. Did you know The Book of Revelation prophesied the internet, computers, television, cell phones and satellite communications? That's right! It does. In Revelation 11:3-12 the Bible tells us that two prophets will be openly preaching against the future World Dictator in Jerusalem. He'll get so upset with them after a while that he will have them killed and leave their bodies to rot on display in the streets of Jerusalem. Then this dictator will allow the TV News and Press to setup cameras around their bodies and broadcast that grizzly scene to the world for three and one half days. Scriptures go on to tell us that that scene is seen by men from every people, tribe, language and nation who will gaze on their bodies. Now think on that for a moment. Remember this was written almost 2000 years ago. This is the only generation that has access to video broadcast news feeds on our computers, TVs, and cellphones. In no other time could this prophecy have been fulfilled.

So our knowledge and our ability to apply it to technology has brought about an explosion of knowledge in the last 100 years. But I still find it amazing that programmers sat down and worked with NASA using all their accumulated historic data as well as access to current data. This was done to develop a computer program that can project planet movement in the future as well as the distant past. This latter ability of the program is giving us amazing insights into past Biblical events and what was happening with the planets and constellations during those events.

God said, "Let there be lights in the vault of the sky to separate the day from the night, and let them serve as signs to mark sacred times, and days and years." Genesis 1:14 *(I believe this is in reference to turning the lights back on that were turned off by Him in Jeremiah 4:28. Genesis like many books in the Bible such as Daniel, Isaiah, Jeremiah, Ezekiel, Revelation etc. have reference to Past, Present and Future time periods in the same verses. It takes knowledge of the Bible, Patience and the Holy Spirit to recognize these time shifts. I believe this was done on purpose by God to confuse the fallen angels when they read the scriptures and also to encourage us to comply with Joshua 1:8)*

> 1 Peter 1:12 Unto whom it was revealed, that not unto themselves, but unto us they did minister the things, which are now reported unto you by them that have preached the gospel unto you with the Holy Ghost sent down from heaven; which things the angels desire to look into.

We must remember that Satan wants to know God's plans so he can work against them and he knows the Bible is full of prophecies. All of which can't be understood fully without the help of the Holy Spirit.

'The Heavens declare the glory of God; the skies proclaim the work of His hands. Day after day they pour forth speech; night after night they reveal knowledge. They have no speech, they use no words; no sound is heard from them. Yet their voice goes out into all the Earth, their words to the ends of the world.' Psalm 19:1-4 *(This was also happening in the first creation event of Genesis 1:1. I must note here that God's story only comes forth with the original interpretation for each constellation that was given to Adam. Not the daily horoscopes that so many follow regularly.)*

Jeremiah 8:2 They will be exposed to the sun and the moon and all the stars of the heavens, which they have loved and served and which they have followed and consulted and worshiped *(Their daily horoscopes which have prevented God's message in the stars.)*. They will not be gathered up or buried, but will be like dung lying on the ground.

What is God saying here? Well He's saying that the stars, planets and constellations were designed by Him to mark sacred times, and days and years Genesis 1:14. Not to forecast your future. He's also conveying the fact that He put the constellations together and oriented planet Earth so everyone on Earth could plainly see the story He is telling with pictures in the night sky. We must remember that the Jewish calendar is different from the one we use today. Theirs has only 360 days as opposed to our 365 day calendar. The Jewish year is marked by seven annual feasts which God instituted. They are (Pesach) Passover, Unleavened Bread, First Fruits, (Shavuot) Pentecost, (Rosh HaShanah) Feast of Trumpets, (Yom Kippur) Day of Atonement, and (Sukkot) Feast of Tabernacles. According to Leviticus 23 the Passover begins on the eve of Nissan 14 when the Jews are to eat the Sedar meal.

The Sedar is celebrated the eve before the lambs are to be killed. This is the meal Jesus ate with His disciples before He was arrested in the Garden of Gethsemane. We also have to remember that the Jewish day goes from 6PM to the next day at 6PM. The Jewish month of Nissan begins when two priests confirm that they both saw a full moon. When this happens they begin their first month, Nissan, of their calendar year which occurs in March-April of our calendar. Please remember that we added 5 more days to our calendar and that's why Nissan can fall in either March or April. At any rate God wanted the Jews to be conscious of what was happening in the night sky. Please keep in mind that 2,000 years ago there was no light pollution so the moon, stars and constellations were extremely visible to the naked eye of everyone on Earth.

As we will see moving forward from here is that what God said in Psalm 91:1-4 was true as He did lay out the story of Jesus in the constellations. These constellations have been extremely stable for the last 6,000 years of recorded history. They were already in place (telling their story) before

Lucifer reigned here on Earth (Ezekiel 28:2-18; Jeremiah 4:22-28; Isaiah 14:13-14). We saw the evidence for this with the three different sets of pyramids which are all perfectly aligned to Orion's Belt. This stability shows that the Big Bang Theory, which states that the planets, suns and galaxies were all formed by accidental rock collisions and that nothing was designed, which is false. It is pure Hogwash, as we use to say. You'll see, very soon, there is no way to deny Intelligent Design and you'll forever reject the World's Big Bang Theory as just plain nonsense. Now we've seen that God has told us He placed a story in the night skies that He wants everyone to see and understand, because it reveals the Glory of God.

By the end of this chapter you will understand that the Glory of God is Jesus and His mission here on Earth. This is so important to God that He keyed the Hebrew calendar up in such a way that the Jews would be forced to watch the night sky. So they could observe the movements of the constellations in order to keep their calendar and the seven feasts that mark their calendar's progress through every year. However the Jews were not the only ones observing the stars' movements. Legend has it that Adam explained the story in the stars to Cain, Abel and Seth. The legend says that Seth explained it to Enoch and he spread this knowledge far and wide before he was taken to Heaven. We find this explained in the Apocrypha Book of Enoch.

Over the centuries the Devil perverted this knowledge and we find that perversion in the practice of horoscope reading from which people try to predict the future. This practice will not work out well for them and we know this from reading God's warning to them in Jeremiah 8:2, which speaks of their final end. God does not want His creation used improperly so His warning is not for a pretty outcome. He created the zodiac constellations to tell the story about the Glory of God, Jesus. Today they have been grossly misrepresented and used to falsely forecast people's future. Those that ascribe to this wrong belief system will end as God told them through the Prophet Jeremiah. God uses the planets and stars for His purposes and here is a perfect example. Thanks to modern technology in the form of the NASA database and the software that has been developed to access that data we can see exactly what the positions of the stars and planets were on any given date in the past. We just have to adjust those computer generated dates to reflect the 5 day difference between our modern calendar and the traditional Jewish calendar. This is because the NASA program was keyed to our modern calendar.

Now in Matthew 2:2, it states what the three wise men told King Herod 'they had seen his star.' In those days they were called Magi and were probably from Persia or Babylon. They told Herod that they had followed this star and it led them to Jerusalem. Well we know today that stars don't move, but they didn't have that knowledge back then. So what were they following? The Planet Jupiter, The King Planet, as it was known back then. On Sept. 10-12 in 6 BC the Planet Jupiter was going through a retrograde west to east.

A census was ordered by Cesar Augustus in 8-7 BC which forced Joseph and Mary to travel to Bethlehem for this census and Mary was pregnant at that time. Scholars traditionally say Jesus was born around Tishrei 10 5BC, which is during the Jewish New Year and Feast of Rosh Hashanah. This is The Feast of Trumpets. So during the first days of Jesus on Earth the Shofar was blown 100 times during that day. I believe God set this up just to have the Shofar herald in the birth of His Son. We know Herod the Great tried to kill Jesus as a baby in Bethlehem and that Herod died in 4 BC. So Jesus' birth would have to be roughly around 6-5 BC on Tishrei or THE Feast of Trumpets. Remember that the Magi found Jesus as a young child living in a house in Bethlehem according to scripture Matthew 2:11. Definitely not a new born and not in a stable as our traditions have told us. Also this feast of Trumpets in 2023 will be held on September 15th. So once again tradition is lying to us that Jesus was born on December 25th.

Retrograde

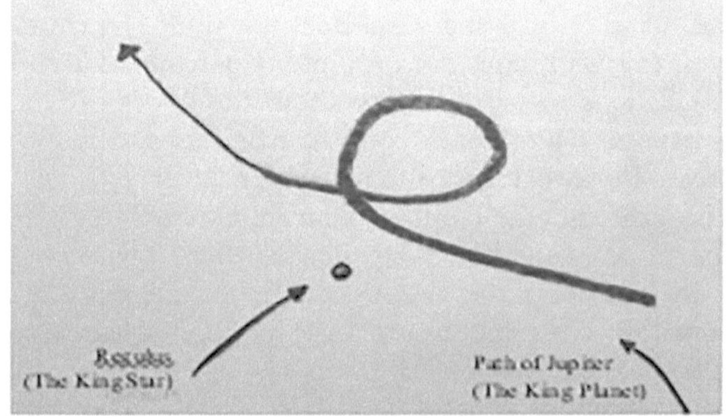

Why did the three wise men or Magi leave their homeland and travel to Jerusalem? Because they saw the planet Jupiter go into Retrograde three times. So what is retrograde? Well Copernicus first observed this change in motion of the planets in the 1500s. Retrograde occurs because of the orbital position of the Earth and the planet in retrograde, which in this case was Jupiter. Retrograde looks like the planet is moving on its course as it normally does. Then it slows down and eventually stops. After this it appears to move backward on its orbital course for a bit. Next it looks like it is slowing down and stopping again. After this it will reverse into its normal speed and direction. From our position on Earth, the retrograde path of the planet is sometimes referred to as a 'halo' or 'crowning' affect. The retrograde motion is not rare or unusual with planets. In fact Mercury goes into retrograde 2 or 3 times a year and Jupiter does it normally once a year. But it usually occurs in open space with no stars around it. So why would this retrograde attract the Magi's attention?

Well there are four reasons.

1. According to NASA this retrograde was done not in open space as usual but in the constellation of Leo the lion. Remember Jesus is also known as the Lion of Judah.

2. Jupiter back then was known as the King Planet.

3. In this retrograde The King Planet Jupiter went into retrograde in the Leo constellation and haloed the star Regulus in that constellation. Back then Regulus was called The Little King. So on September 11, 6 BC (*remember the program is key to our calendar dating not the Jewish calendar*) the King Planet Jupiter haloed The Little King star Regulus in the constellation of Leo. This was very significant to the Magi and it got their attention.

4. And the most unusual aspect of this event is that Jupiter went into retrograde two more times, February 17, 5 BC and again on May 8, 5 BC according to the NASA computer, each time haloing Regulus.

I believe the Magi started packing on February 17, 5 BC and started on their ways toward Jerusalem and their urgency increased when it happened for the third time on May 8, 5 BC. The Magi saw all 3 because they were observing and following, not a star because they don't move, but the planet Jupiter did. This was the sign that the Jewish leaders missed because they weren't observing the constellations the God had intended them to be watching. Only God could put this together and He did it to herald the birth of Jesus His Son. The aspect of retrograde to me seems like God has set up a system that keeps the planets on their proper orbits. The retrograde is the process of resetting their course on a regular bases. Keep in mind that we only know today when these retrogrades happened because of NASA's modern Astrological program. This program can show us what has happened to planets in the past. NASA had the data and talented programmers put them together.

Remember God Prophesied in Daniel 12:4 that in the End Times there would be an explosion of knowledge and this is one of the benefits of that knowledge explosion. So we know through hindsight that this was a sign from God that the Jewish Rabbis should not have missed. Remember they kept asking Jesus for a sign. And we just confirmed that the sign did occur and the Magi did not miss it. Remember the Jewish leaders missed this same event. Now we know why the Magi traveled so far to honor the new king with gifts. These same gifts helped support Jesus and His family in Egypt until Herod died in 4 BC.

I can plainly see God's involvement in this whole story can't you? Now to add insult to injury for the Jewish leaders on September the 11, 6 BC (*remember this date is according to our calendar not the Jewish calendar*) in the night sky over Jerusalem the constellations of Virgo and Draco were visible to those on Earth who were paying attention. How is this relevant? Well the heavens declare the Glory of God. The beginning of the Jewish year is the month of Tishrei. Remember the first day is marked by two Rabbis agreeing there was a full moon. And where did they have to look to find the full moon? Up into the night sky. When their agreement is recorded the Priest gives the order for The Feast of Trumpets too begin. This is the Jewish New Year. On this night 100 Rams Horns or Shofars are blown from the walls of Jerusalem. These horns were to announce the New Year, at other times they were blown for an alarm for war or to coronate a new King. Which of these do you think God intended when they blew this night as Jesus was born in Bethlehem? Remember God set all this up centuries in advance to coronate the New King of Israel who had just been born 6 miles away in a Bethlehem stable, Jesus His Son.

Back to the stars again. In 6-5, BC, according the NASA computer, (*I believe this was 6-5 BC as Herod died in 4 BC*) over Jerusalem the sun was moving through the center of the constellation Virgo, effectively in the woman's belly. All the while the consolation of Virgo was standing directly over the full moon that the two Rabbi witnesses just certified they saw, initiating the Feast of Trumpets. A nearby group of 12 stars between Virgo and Leo were also forming a circular pattern above Virgo's head, something several star charts and books refer to as the diadem, or crowning of Virgo. Today these stars are very difficult to see because of light pollution. The sun, moon and these 12 stars relation to the constellation of Virgo are laid out in Revelation 12 as the sign of the Son of man, Jesus.

Now nearby Virgo is the constellation of Draco in the Zodiac of Dendera, which depicts a dragon that is ready to pounce on and devour the child of the virgin the moment it is born. We know this relationship because we are so told again in Revelation chapter 12. Remember that Revelation is telling of things in the Present, Past and Future and some of the symbolism speaks to more than one time period. Now then as some people speak of meteor showers as shooting or falling stars. So God in Revelation 12 was talking of two different time periods in reference to the dragon's tail causing 1/3 of the stars to fall from heaven. Two different events taking place at two different times in history. The first event occur in the distant past long before Adam and Eve. This book will address that event when the Dragon, Satan, leads 1/3 of the angels and all the humans on the Earth at that time to rebel against God and try to overthrow Him. According to NASA a 3 day meteor shower also occurred around 6-5 BC at Jesus' birth.

The second event is at the birth of Jesus. NASA's computer information shows that on the night of Jesus' birth the Earth was passing through a meteor band and from September 10th to the 12th there was a meteor shower event for 3 days emanating from the area of space where the tail of the constellation of Draco was located. So let's recap. On the night Jesus was born in September around 6-5 BC and we calculate this approximate time because of Herod's death in 4 BC. The constellation of Virgo was overhead with the shadow of the Sun travelling through its center. The full moon (which I would remind you that the two Temple Priests were watching for) appears to be at Virgo's feet. While a small group of 12 stars between Virgo and Leo is crowning the head of Virgo along with an intense meteor shower occurred from the tail area of the Draco constellation. Wow! To add insult to injury all the Jewish leaders missed this sign happening in the night sky above Jerusalem. This story in the stars is explained in Revelation 12 and shows that the dragon (representing Satan) was ready to devour or kill the child Jesus the moment He was born. *(It also demonstrates that even though Satan has great wisdom and knowledge he doesn't know everything. He is also not omni present and can't be everywhere at the same time as God can.)*

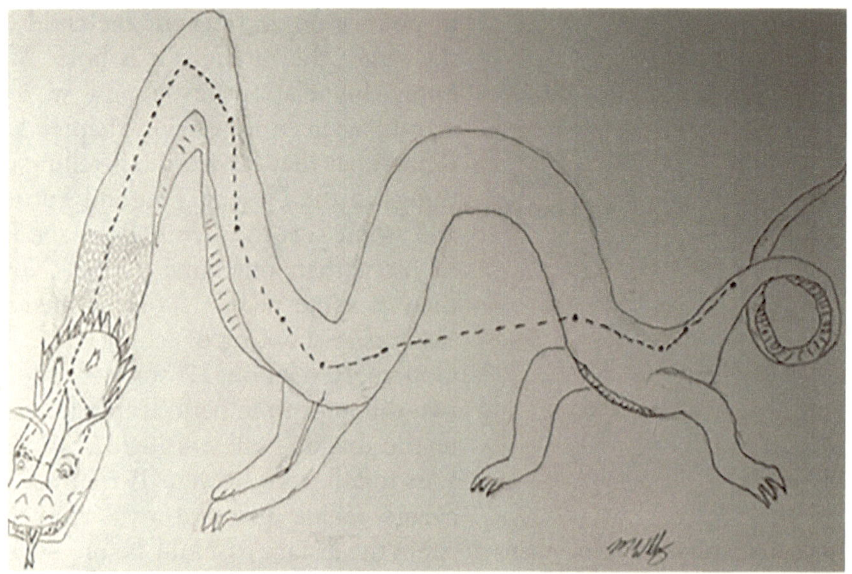

Now remember when the Magi *(Wise Men)* got to Jerusalem, they went straight to Herod to inquire about the child. Why wouldn't they? All the signs in the sky pointed to the fact that this child would be a King in Israel. Herod inquired about when they had seen Jupiter haloing Regulus. Then Herod went to the Jewish Priests and inquired from them where the Messiah was to be born and he was told about the prophecy of the Messiah being born in Bethlehem. Herod went back to the Magi and told them about Bethlehem and asked them to go and honor the new King and then return and tell him where they found Him so that he then could go and honor Him as well.

The Magi went and found Jesus He was a young child (Matthew 2:11) who then was about 1-2 years old and living in a house in Bethlehem. If you haven't figured it out yet, the Christmas fable we celebrate today is wrong. Remember the Magi did not know Herod's reputation, because they had never been to Israel or Jerusalem before. Therefore God sent an angel to warn them about Herod and they went home a different way. Then the angel woke Joseph and Mary and sent them on their way to Egypt that very night. Meanwhile Herod waited for the Magi to do their business and return to him with the information he wanted. When they didn't come back Herod was furious and sent his Mercenaries to Bethlehem with orders to kill every male child 2 and under. They followed their orders that bloody night and the Bible says Rachel mourned in Israel fulfilling another Prophecy. (Jeremiah 31:15)

Notice the story the stars are telling with Virgo giving birth and Draco crouching ready to pounce on the child came true and at the very same time 100 Shofars were being blown from the top of Jerusalem's walls. Now most would ignore this but I believe the 100 Rams Horns, the Shofars, in God's eyes were being blown to usher in King Jesus. Please also think about all of these events, the 3 Magi in Persia saw the sign from God and acted upon it while the religious elite of Israel all missed it. Only Anna and Simeon recognized the Messiah when He was brought to the Temple for circumcision to enter the Abrahamic Covenant. WOW!

Now Jesus always celebrated all the Feasts and when He started His ministry He continued with this practice. On the Feast of Tabernacles He went to the Temple and on the last day of the Feast. During this feast a priest always carried an empty jug to the Pool of Siloam. This is a spring which has a pool filled pure water used for ritual cleansing in the Temple. At the Pool the priest fills the jug with the living water from the pool and carries it back to the Temple. In the Temple the living water is poured over the Alter cleansing it. There are only three sources of living water according to Jewish tradition: rivers, rain and springs. As we see in scripture, John 7:37, Jesus stood up in the Temple on the last and greatest day of this festival when this takes place. Jesus stood and said in a loud voice, 'Let anyone who is thirsty come to me and drink.' All this was happening while the constellation of Aquarius was in the sky above Jerusalem. Jesus was tying Himself to the Aquarius constellation. Earlier in John the scriptures say that Jesus timed His departure from Galilee to arrive in Jerusalem at the precise time the request for living water was made. Remember, the Aquarius constellation is pouring out his living water into the mouth of the fish. Only God could be so precise in His timing.

Now we've seen how God has used the planets, stars, sun, moon, and constellations to mark the birth of Jesus. So let's see what else the story in the stars tell us. Keep in mind that God set all this up when He created the Universe in the distant past. That was before Lucifer (Satan) rebelled and caused the destruction of all living things in the first flood. This was long before Adam and Eve were created. Talk about long term planning. Today the Chinese have a 100 year plan, but their forward planning is minuscule compared to God's. As a matter of fact it looks kind of juvenile in comparison.

We know these constellations were in place before Lucifer ruled Earth and this is proven from Archeology as well. As you'll see in the chapter on Megalithic Construction Lucifer used his knowledge and advanced technology to build his cities and nations many thousands of years ago. You'll see evidence of construction techniques we would have difficulty duplicating today. But that ancient construction (in many cases) was keyed to the positions of the constellations. Example; The pyramids at Xian China, Teotihuacan Mexico and The Great pyramids in Giza, Egypt are all keyed to Orion's Belt. I don't think this is a coincidence and as you'll see they were all built before Adam.

The constellation of ARA represents an altar of fire, which is located just below the constellation of CRAX or as it is commonly known as the Southern Cross. Now the flames in ARA are blowing away from the Southern Cross. This is like the wind of the Holy Spirit is shouting from the Cross saying 'The people who believe in Jesus and His sacrifice for them are free from the judgment of fire. They are under Grace not the Law!' I love that ancient interpretation! Let's move on to the constellations of CENTAURUS and LUPUS, which are located just above the Southern Cross and ARA. Remember that God is telling a story with pictures here and that the meanings of the constellations were explained to Adam who told his sons Able, Cain and Seth. Seth in turn explained them to Enoch who spread the information far and wide before he was taken to heaven. *(According to The Book of Enoch)*

Also remember God is using symbolism here to tell this story. This is reminiscent of the symbols He has used in dreams and visions to convey messages to people. In Pharaoh's dream about seven years of plentiful harvest and seven years of famine, but none of the wise men of Egypt could interpret his dream. Then God gave Joseph the interpretation. (Gen 41:1-48) The Centaur represents a two natured figure of man and God, in other words Jesus. The Centaur is piercing the constellation of Lupus with a spear, Lupus represents Satan. Okay, these two constellations are located over the Southern Cross or the CRAX constellation and the ARA or fiery altar constellation. In other words Jesus will defeat Satan through the Cross and save those that believe in Him from judgment. Right above the constellation of Centaurus is the constellation of LIBRA, which represent the scales of heaven. This should remind us of Daniel 5:27 'You have been weighed on the scales and found wanting.' A scary thought for all, but keep in mind Jesus paid our debt on the cross and for all who believe in Him the fires of judgment have been turned away from us.

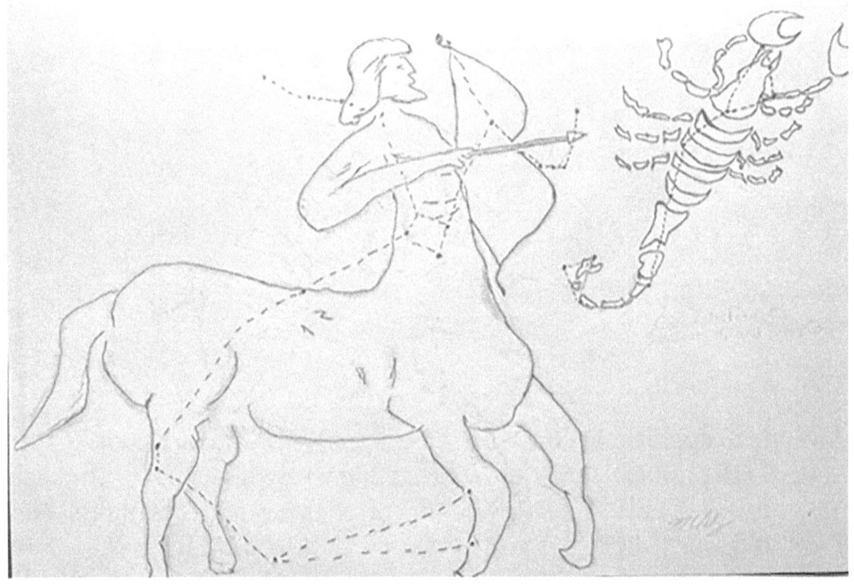

Moving on a little beyond LIBRA is the constellation of CORONA. It is a small constellation, but it is the great crown of heaven, quite fitting for the King of Kings. This group of constellations shows the God Man, Jesus, pierce Satan with a spear, while His death on the cross frees us from the eternal fire of judgment and now He wears a glorious crown and holds the scale of judgment forever. In the constellations of SAGITTARIUS and SCORPIO we again see the two natured representation of God and Man in the form of a Centaur. Here we see SAGITTARIUS holding a bow and arrow ready to shoot the constellation of SCORPIO which represents Satan. Different pictures but repeating the story. Pounding home 1John 3:8b 'The reason the Son of God appeared was to destroy the Devil's work.'

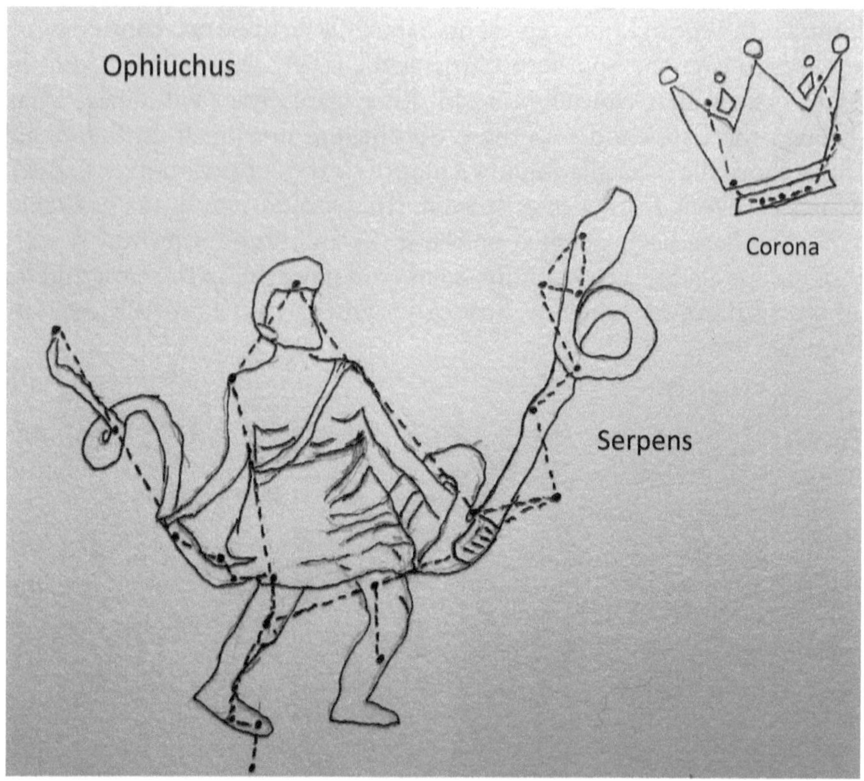

I love the next group of constellations. The OPHIUCHUS constellation depicts a tall powerful man, Jesus, struggling with a huge snake. The snake constellation is called SERPENS and of course represents Satan. Now SERPENS looks like it is trying to reach CORONA, which is the Crown of Heaven. But under OPHIUCHUS is the constellation of SCORPIO and from the positioning of these constellations it looks like SCORPIO is about to sting the heel of ORPHIUCHUS and ORPHIUCHUS' foot is above the head of SCORPIO. So here we have a pictorial of Jesus holding back Satan from stealing the crown of Heaven while Satan is trying to sting Jesus' heel and Jesus is about to crush Satan's head. Keep in mind that Satan has been trying to get the Crown of Heaven since long before Adam and Eve came to life in Genesis. Getting the Crown was the motive for his rebellion when he led 1/3 of the angels and all the people on the Earth during that time period. He lost of course and we'll get into that later on in this book.

These constellations are depicting Genesis 3:15 'And I will put enmity between thee and the woman, and between thy seed and her seed; it shall bruise thy head, and thou shalt bruise his heel.' That was God speaking to Satan in the Garden of Eden. Psalm 6:21 'Surely God will crush the heads of His enemies.' Revelation 19:16 'On His robe and on His thigh He has this written: King of Kings and Lord of Lords.' Now we come to the constellation of BOOTES. It depicts a man, Jesus, who is holding a spear and his left arm is raised holding a sickle. It is in motion ready to cut off the head of SERPENS should it reach the crown of CORONA. The message here is that Satan the serpent is obstructed and defeated from every possible angle.

Let's continue. Our small solar system is located in the Milky Way. There are two arms to this spiral galaxy and we are located in what's known as the Orion Arm. Our solar system is located perfectly to allow us an excellent view of the stars and constellations that we now know God has set in place from the beginning of creation to reveal the Glory of God, which is Jesus, to the entire world. The constellation of ORION has the figures of a warrior with raised club and holding a shield that resembles a lion's head. Revelation 5:5 'Then one of the elders said to me, 'Do not weep! See, the Lion of the tribe of Judah, the Root of David, has triumphed. He is able to open the scroll and its seven seals.'

Orion

But ORION is more than the shield. The word Orion means light in Hebrew and many cultures refer to him as the light bearer. Remember how Jesus tied Himself to AQUARIUS? Here He does the same thing with ORION. John 8:12 'When Jesus spoke again to the people, He said, "I'm the light of the world. Whoever follows me will never walk in darkness, but will have the light of life." This also ties in with the statement at the beginning of John about John the Baptist. John 1:6-8 'There was a man sent from God, whose name was John. The same came for a witness of the Light, that all men through Him might believe. He was not that Light, but was sent to bear witness of that Light.' John was baptizing at Bethabara beyond Jordan when he saw Jesus coming. John 1:29-30 The next day John saw Jesus coming unto him, and said, 'Behold the Lamb of God, which takes away the sin of the world. This is He of whom I said, After me comes a man which is preferred before me; for He was before me.' The next day John pointed Jesus out to two of his disciples, James and John and said, 'behold the Lamb of God' and those disciples followed Jesus.

The ancients Jews believed that ORION was a picture of the Messiah, the conquering Messiah and if you remember the constellations depict the Messiah out to kill Satan. But the constellations also show the cross and flaming altar, CRUX *(Southern Cross)* and ARA *(the flaming altar)*. I believe that the OPHINCHUS constellation, which shows the Messiah holding back the snake *(Satan)* from taking the heavenly crown (the CORONA constellation) represents our current position in the story. Jesus, through His church, is holding Satan back and disrupting his plans. John 12:46 'I have come into the world as a light, so that no one who believes in me should stay in darkness.' This is telling us that the darkness would still be here for a while, but those that believe in Jesus could be free of the darkness and would be equipped to fight against it.

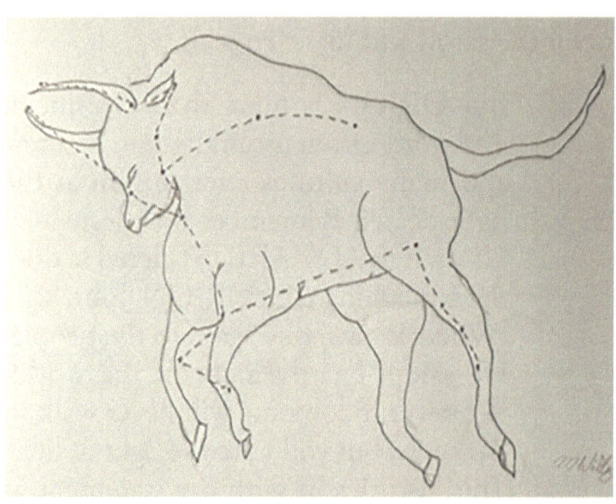
Taurus

TAURUS is directly above the constellation of CETUS which is the great beast who holds the constellation of PISCES in chains. The TAURUS constellation is always looking like it is in motion charging toward CETUS. Again the repetition of good fighting evil is here repeated by God. There are two star clusters in the constellation of TAURUS, Pleiades and Hyades, their names in Greek both mean 'rain'. Another connection to living water for the Messiah. Jesus employed a unique teaching method called REMEZ. It was known in His time as the hinting method. It worked back then because every child had to memorize the Tanakh *(which is the Hebrew Bible and Christian's Old Testament)*. Whoever wanted to say something without saying it out loud would give their audience a hint that would cause them to recognize the portion of scripture you were speaking about.

So when Jesus said He was the Son of Man, they would have recognized the Messianic reference to what was written in Daniel 7:13-14 'In my vision I looked, and there before me was one like the son of man, coming with the clouds of heaven. He approached the ancient of days and was led into His presence. He was given authority, glory and sovereign power; all nations and people of every language worshipped Him. His dominion is an everlasting dominion that will not pass away, and His kingdom is one that will never be destroyed.'

Jesus employed this language in Matthew 24. He called Himself the bread of life. His audience would have known from scripture that the Messiah, the Root of David was to be born in Bethlehem where King David had been born. They also would have known that the Hebrew meaning of Bethlehem is "house of bread" and *(now this is very interesting)* all the lambs used as Passover sacrifices had to be born in Bethlehem. According to Rabbinic writings lambs born and raised in Bethlehem were used for Temple sacrifices. The daily Temple sacrifice required two unblemished sheep from Bethlehem. One sacrificed in the morning and one for evening sacrifice. One year old lambs were also needed for Passover and other festivals. WOW! So God set all these rules up long before Jesus that all sacrificial lambs had to be born in Bethlehem. Precisely why Cesar could be inspired to take a census which forced Joseph and Mary to travel to Bethlehem. So Jesus was born there and therefore He could be God's sacrificial Lamb on Passover some 33 years after birth.

Did you tie that together in your minds along with everything else God setup for that one moment in time? He used the planets He created to attract the Magi's attention. When Jupiter *(the King Planet)* in retrograde crowned Regulus *(the little king planet)* not once but three times in the constellation of LEO. It was God who initiated the seven Feasts of the Lord. In Leviticus 23 God laid out these feast for Israel to follow each year and the feasts controlled their calendar as well. Passover, Unleavened Bread, First Fruits, Pentecost, Trumpets, Atonement and Tabernacles. Holy and sacred times that God initiated and if the Jewish leaders of His time had been paying attention they would have seen the signs from God that marked Jesus as the Messiah. Remember all through Jesus' ministry, they kept asking Him for a sign and at the same time they kept missing them. I realize that hindsight is much better but come on talk about the blind leading the blind.

CAPRICORN is an image of two different animals, a goat and a fish. Throughout scripture bulls, goats, rams and lambs are the animals most often used for sacrifice. During the sacred day of Yom Kippur, which is also known as the Day of Atonement, the ceremony laid out in Leviticus 16:6-10 was to take place. 'Aaron is to offer the bull for his own sin offering to make atonement for himself and his household. Then he is to take two goats and present them before the Lord at the entrance to the tent of meeting. He is to cast lots for the two goats - one lot for the Lord and the other for the scapegoat. Aaron shall bring the goat whose lot falls to the Lord and sacrifice it for a sin offering. But the goat chosen by lot as the scapegoat shall be presented alive before the Lord to be used for making Atonement by sending it into the wilderness as a scapegoat. The Priest was to lay hands on the goat thereby symbolically transferring the sins of Israel to it then release it into the wilderness where it would die.'

However the priests did not trust that this goat could not find its way back to the city so they hired a Gentile to take it out into the wilderness and push it off a cliff backwards. The reason they hired a Gentile for this task was because he was a non-believer so if the sins transferred to him then he was already full of sin so no big deal. The sacrificial goat paid in blood for the sins of the people but the scapegoat carried the sins away from the people and the city. Just as Jesus did for us.

> 1 Peter 2:24 'He Himself bore our sins in His body on the cross, so that we might die to sins and live for righteousness; by His wounds we are healed.'

Now it's interesting to remember that it was the priests of Israel who handed Jesus over to the Romans *(Gentiles)* who then took Him outside the city walls to a hill called Golgotha where they killed Him. Sound familiar? So let's look at the second half of CAPRICORN. It is a fish, a bit puzzling I agree. However, at least 10 other cultures use the fish as a symbol for life. Here it symbolizes the goat's transition through death to life through the resurrection and keep in mind God was speaking to the whole Earth about the Messiah. Remember as well that the early church used the symbol of the fish to represent Jesus and some of us have taken that up again.

Something that is not commonly known is that Ron Wyatt in January of 1982 discovered the Ark of the Covenant in Jeremiah's Grotto near the foot of Golgotha Hill outside of Jerusalem. It was turned over to the Israeli authorities and remains hidden and out of sight. He did this by following a lead that he discovered in The Book of Maccabees, 2 Maccabees 2:5-8. It speaks of Jeremiah taking the sacred vessels of the Temple to a place that was prepared by Solomon for just that purpose. This was done as the Babylonian army in 586 BC was approaching the city of Jerusalem. In this cave Jeremiah placed the Tent, the Ark and the Altar of Incense. Then he sealed up the entrance. The Book of Maccabees also says 'God declared 'The place shall remain unknown until God gathers His people together again and shows them mercy. (This happened in 1948 when Israel became a nation) The Book of Maccabees was written 150 years before Jesus and remained in the Bible until it was removed in 1824 with other books of the Apocryphal.

This had to be God. I say that because this hiding place was exactly 20 feet below the base of the cross that Jesus was crucified on. We have to grasp the magnificence of this, because God kept Jeremiah's Grotto hidden for 2569 years. Things that were hidden are now being revealed in this the last generation before Jesus returns.

> Colossians 2:**14** Blotting out the handwriting of ordinances that was against us, which was contrary to us, and took it out of the way, nailing it to his cross (God was at the cross with the handwriting of ordinances that were against us and He nailed it to Jesus' cross. No one saw God doing this but scripture tells us that He did. No one comes to Him without faith in Jesus)

> John 19:30; Matthew 27:**50** Jesus, when he had cried again with a loud voice 'It is finished', He yielded up the ghost. **51** And, behold, the veil of the temple was rent in twain from the top to the bottom; and the Earth did quake, and the rocks rent;

When this quake struck as Jesus died and the Centurion speared His side causing the blood and water to gush out. A fissure was formed in the Golgotha Hill that ran to its base, but a smaller fissure ran from the base of the cross down through the rock to the hidden chamber carrying the blood of Jesus to the Mercy Seat on the Ark of the Covenant. This dried blood was still there when Ron Wyatt found it in 1982 and he had it tested. By a miracle it was still viable and showed it contained only 23 chromosomes and one Y chromosome. The testing facility told him a baby usually receives 23 chromosomes from each parent, but these 23 were from the mother's side, giving all the physical characteristics and the one Y chromosome made Him male but it wasn't from a human. We know it was from God and He set all of this up.

Gemini

Alright let's move on to the constellation of GEMINI. In the ancient star maps it is always depicted as twin boys, but with our politically correct society of late it has been depicted as twin girls or girl and boy. The ancient maps show God's original meaning, twin boys. One in front carrying a harp and one in back carrying a weapon. Now this constellation depicts the appearances of Jesus. First the one with the harp. The harp represents peace and it was David's favorite instrument. Jesus' first coming was to bring peace and reconciliation to men from God. His second coming is to bring war and the destruction of His enemies. Hosea 6:3 depicts the separate comings as seasons.

'Let us acknowledge the Lord; let us press on to acknowledge him. As surely as the sun rises, he will appear; he will come to us like the winter rains, like the spring rains that water the Earth.'

Please note that the winter rains and the spring rains are at the opposite ends of the calendar separated by a period of time. In our case it will be over 2,000 years. But remember in God's time zone that's only 2 days.

> 2 Peter 3/8 KJV - But, beloved, be not ignorant of this one thing, that one day is with the Lord as a thousand years, and a thousand years as one day.

The constellation of LEO has three deacons. A deacon is a smaller constellation and always near to a larger constellation and in this case LEO. Leo's three deacons are HYDRA which depicts a snake, CRATER depicts a bowl leaning to the side like something was being poured out and it is located near the center of HYDRA. Finally there is CORVUS a raven, a bird of prey. These are located under the constellation of LEO, which is always depicted as a crouching lion ready to pounce on HYDRA.

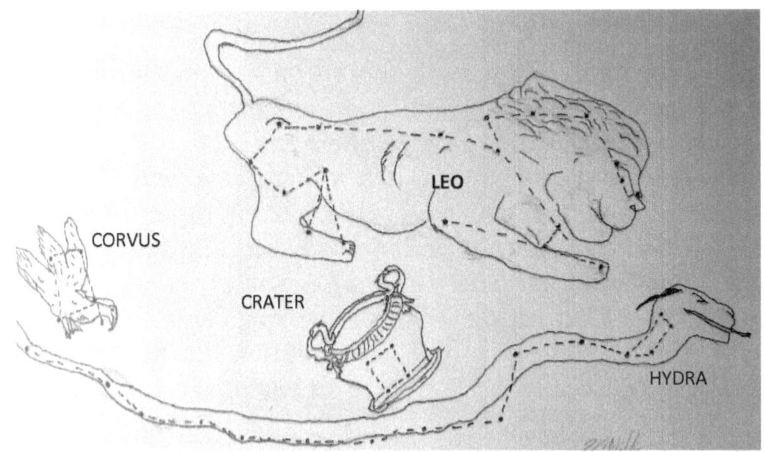

Rev 5:5 'See, the Lion of the tribe of Judah, the root of David, has triumphed.'

Remember, Jesus returns to Earth on the final day of the Tribulation. He comes at the end of a horrible 7 year period on Earth. During the latter part of this period of time, Satan has moved two armies toward each other. The army of the Antichrist has taken over Israel through invasion from his stronghold in Europe. At the same time, a 200-million-man army from Asia has been fighting its way toward the Antichrist's army, killing 1/3 of the Earth's population on the way. Most recently, God has poured out His seven last plagues on the world, this is depicted by CRATER the pouring bowl. During the last few weeks of this mighty struggle, God will call every available bird from the four corners of the Earth into the area of the Valley of Jehoshaphat in Israel. The birds are depicted by CORVUS which is picking at the tail of HYDRA. These birds will clean up the Battlefield of Armageddon.

On the very last day of the seven years of Tribulation, a bright light will come from the east. The clashing armies of the Antichrist and the 200 million man army of Asia will see the penetrating bright light that is piercing the darkness they have lived in for three days. As the light broadens and becomes brighter, yet they will see millions of white horses with riders, all dressed in pure white garments, charging toward them on the clouds. The lead rider will be dressed in vestments of red and gold. For a moment, their terrible battle has come to a halt. They once again begin to take notice of the searing heat from the sun, but they all still stare mesmerized by the ever expanding light on the horizon. Suddenly, the lead rider holds up His arm and the whole charging procession comes to a halt.

They hear Him speak a few words toward them, not knowing it was a plague on them. Suddenly, and I mean instantaneously, the flesh begins to melt from the bodies after their eyes have melted in their sockets. The flesh slides from every living creature on that battle field and all those associated with those armies in any way. The blood rushes to the ground so fast and in such volume that the Earth beneath their feet cannot absorb it and it rises to the height of a horses bridle over the entire Plains of Armageddon. When all are dead Jesus gives a command and all the billions of birds begin the gruesome task of cleaning the battle field. Then begins the 1,000 year reign of Jesus here on Earth.

The Crucifixion

Again let's remember that God said the sun, moon and stars would mark the holy days and feasts, which He laid out in Leviticus 23. He also told Moses to slaughter a lamb or ram. Remember that God supplied the ram to Abraham for sacrifice in the place of his son Isaac at Mount Moriah (which is in the Jerusalem area). Now, with this knowledge, the fact that the constellation of ARIES is above Jerusalem in the night sky, every year, at the Feast of Passover and we know that ARIES portrays a ram. The sun, moon and stars not only mark the feast days, but they also are used to mark the days and years in the Jewish calendar. We have been warned by God in Jeremiah 8:2 not to worship the stars or use them to forecast future events. But people today, even some Christians, are drawn toward this and it's called astrology. More commonly known as horoscopes. God plainly warned people that He would leave the people that use this practice behind, like dung on the ground when the time comes if they are believing and following after Astrology *(Horoscopes)*. God's attitude on sin does not change. So my friends stay away from that stuff like the plague.

Jesus used the stars, sun and moon as His clock and calendar. Here's what I mean in Matthew 26:2 'As you know, the Passover is two days away and the Son of Man will be handed over to be crucified.' How did He know it was two days away? He had no cell phone, no computer or TV broadcasts giving Him a countdown to Passover. It was because He watched the movement of the stars at night and ARIES was almost over Jerusalem.

We also know it was Jesus' intention to have the Passover with His disciples before He had to go to the Cross. Now when I first became a Christian and was reading this in the Bible I thought Jesus meant eating the whole Passover meal with the lamb and everything else that goes with it. But later when I started studying history and Jewish traditions and applied them toward what I was reading in the Bible I discovered I had been wrong in my assumption. It was the Seder meal He wanted to eat with His disciples. This takes place the night before the sacrificial Lambs are slaughtered in the morning. To the Jews it is the same day as their days run from 6pm to 6pm the following day.

This is the system God set up for the Jews, a calendar with 360 days, the Feasts and when their days started 6pm and ended 6pm. To us today this is the next day, but to the Jews it is the same day. It sounds strange to us, but on the same day that started at 6pm when the sun sets the Passover Lambs are slaughtered, sacrificial goats' lots are drawn and this selects which goat is chosen for their roles by the priests. One is to be sacrificed and the other is the scapegoat, which is laid hands on by the priest for sin transfer and then turned over to a Gentile to take outside the city and be killed. Well, did you see it? Did you get that sudden *Ahaaa* moment?

Let's trace Jesus' day. He got to Jerusalem, they found the upper room, prepared the Seder meal, ate the Seder meal and Jesus added a couple of new steps, went to Gethsemane to pray, He was arrested there and brought to the Temple for trial. The Priests tried Him all night and through false testimony found Him guilty (even though He had never sinned) just like the goats he was chosen to die by the Priests. The Priest then took Him to Pilate early in the morning and past Jesus to the Roman Gentiles to be removed from the city and killed. Sound familiar? Jesus was God's Passover Lamb and God's scapegoat all in one.

Let's recap what we have learned in this chapter:

1. The Magi were attracted to the retrograde activity of the King Planet Jupiter which was haloing the star Regulus which was known at that time as the Little King star. God made this happen three times as the Magi travelled perhaps two years to get to Jerusalem. Remember the Jewish Priests who were supposed to

be paying attention to the sun, moon and stars missed this entirely.

2. We learned that the constellation of VIRGO was in the night sky above Jerusalem and the shadow of the sun was passing through the middle, approximately at her belly. There was a glorious full moon, which two Priests attested too in order to start the Feast of Trumpets, and the full moon they were looking at was directly under the feet of VIRGO. Along with this a group of 12 stars located between VIRGO and LEO had just created a diadem or crown around the head of VIRGO. While at the same time a 3 day meteor shower was flowing out of the tail of the constellation of DRACO fulfilling Revelation 12. That must have been quite a sight, but for some reason these Priests missed all this activity entirely.

3. Through tradition, set up by God, on this night to bring in the Jewish New Year, 100 Rams Horns or Shofars were being blown on the walls of Jerusalem. The Shofars were also blown to commemorate a New King. Jesus was being born in Bethlehem just 6 miles away and the noise of these 100 Shofars would have been clearly herd at that distance during this time in history.

4. Remember in Revelation 12, we saw, through John's interpretation of the constellations VIRGO and DRACO, that Satan was waiting for Jesus to be born so he could kill Him immediately. We saw this play out when the Magi appeared close to two years later and told Herod what they had seen. As we read the Magi went to a house in Bethlehem and not a stable as our traditions portray it. This also took place in September not December. An Angel warned the Magi not to go back to Herod and they went another way. This Angel also warned Joseph to flee to Egypt until Herod was dead and thanks to the Magi's gifts, the family had more than enough financial means to do just that. God executes His plans very well. Satan through Herod sent mercenaries to Bethlehem that night and they killed every male child 2 years and

under, just to be sure. But they were too late. Joseph and his family had already fled the city for Egypt.

5. Prophecies showed that for the Messiah to be from the Root of King David He had to be born in Bethlehem. We also learned that Jewish tradition states all Passover Lambs had to be born in Bethlehem. So naturally this is where God saw to it that He was born. Usually back then, people would almost spend their whole lives in the area of their birth, but because of the Devil's persecution, Jesus spent a few years in Egypt and then the family moved to Galilee. So with this insight now we can see why the Priests and Sadducees kept saying no Prophet or Messiah comes from Galilee. They assumed Jesus was born there not just raised there. Big mistake on their part.

6. We also saw Jesus tie Himself through His sermons to the constellations and now we know that they reveal God's story to everyone on Earth. It's just a shame that we today cannot enjoy seeing them for ourselves because of light pollution.

7. There are a couple of additional facts about the crucifixion you need to know. When Judas left the Seder he went straight to the Priests and for 30 pieces of silver he told them where Jesus would be that night. The Priests sent their men to arrest Him. Then they put Him in a mock trial all night and then turned Him over to the Gentiles *(the Romans)* for them to execute Him. At the same time the ARIES constellation was over Jerusalem and while the Priests were slaughtering the Passover Lambs and selecting the sacrificial goat and scapegoat in the Temple. The Romans had taken Jesus and two thieves outside the city walls to a hill called Galgatha and crucified Him. Matthew 27:45 'from noon until three in the afternoon darkness over all the land.'

8. NASA could not confirm a solar eclipse at that time in history but they confirmed a partial lunar eclipse took place on April 3, AD 28 and lasted 2hrs and 50 minutes. *(Date is adjusted to allow for the 5 day difference*

between the Jewish calendar. Tradition tells us Jesus was 33 when he died and because He was born roughly in 5 BC before Herod the Great died in 4 BC) We have to look at the Greek word used for darkness here and it is Skotos, which comes from another Greek word Skia. This word means shading of light occurred, not complete darkness. So it was a lunar eclipse not a solar eclipse that marked the crucifixion of Jesus.

9. Also at 3pm in the sky above Jerusalem the sun was directly under the foot of the constellation of ARIES. I am sure that Father God meant it to be a reflection of His son Jesus the Lamb of God being crushed on the cross. I'm not going to write out here what crucifixion does to the body but it is an excruciatingly slow way to die. Look it up and read it for yourself. It will give you more appreciation of what Jesus suffered to save us.

10. Let's move on. Jesus rose from the grave on the third day and did some things in Jerusalem, but then went away. He then met with His disciples and about 500 followers for 40 days. John said if all He taught them was written down in books they would fill the world. So let's look back at the stars and see what God is saying and so we have the constellation of PISCES. PISCES depicts two fish held together by a chain. Remember the significance of the fish representing rebirth or new life in that culture back then. Also that early Christians used the image of a fish as their symbol faith, much as we use the cross today.

11. The two fish in PISCES represent sin and death and they are held together through a chain used to hold them captive by the great creature constellation of CETUS. At the crucifixion, VENUS, the Bright

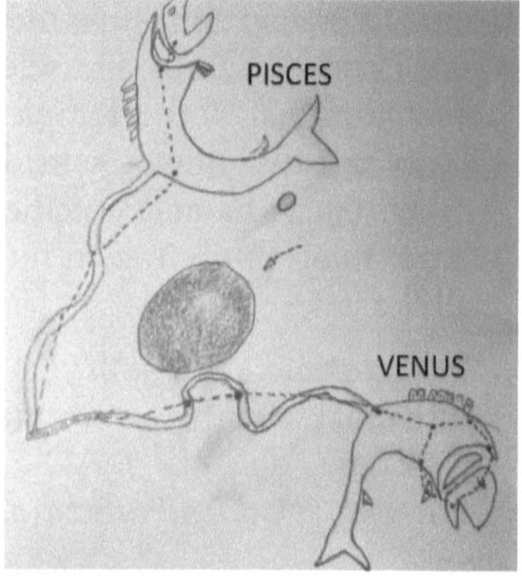

Morning Star, Jesus, was in the center of PISCES constellation as if held captive. This was on April 3, 28 AD, but it continued on normal trajectory until April 11 when it went into retrograde. It started to slow down and gave the appearance of reversing course. On May 6th, 28 AD, it continued its retrograde and broke through the chain holding PISCES prisoner. Psalm 107:14 'He brought them out of darkness, the utter darkness, and broke away their chains.' This coincides with the date of Jesus' ascension into heaven after defeating the enemy and training His disciples for 40 days. WOW!

CHAPTER 7

Hidden Angels

Now that we have investigated the hidden truth about Lucifer's Forgotten Civilization in Chapter 2, it's time to look at how the Bible describes the physical appearance of God's angels. Then, we'll compare how they are portrayed in ancient stories and carved images around the world. Let's start with the Sumerian Kings List which states their first 8 kings ruled for a combined period of 241,000 years. At first glance that would seem to be an impossible length of time for 8 kings to live. However we must keep in mind that these first 8 kings were not human but fallen angels during Lucifer's reign. Let's be mindful that they were created in God's dimension where time is much different than here on Earth. One of their days equals a thousand of our years. So the time span for these first 8 kings of 241,000 years was only 241 days in an angel's life span.

> 2 Peter 3:8
>
> But, beloved, do not forget this one thing, that with the
> Lord one day *is* as a thousand years, and a thousand years
> as one day.

I ask you to use your imagination for a minute and look at how far humans have progressed in 6,000 years after starting from scratch. Now imagine how far Lucifer's society advanced in 241,000 years. We also have to consider the fact that they had the advantage of advanced technologies, which came with Lucifer. Remember that those angels knew the knowledge of the lower secrets of Heaven. That was their starting point. Now with that new information imagine how far that civilization could have progressed in that Sumerian timeframe.

These facts (among other things) are the missing link to understanding Earth's true history. Without understanding this timeline and the Biblical account of Lucifer's rule here on Earth the experts could only interpret what they were finding from a human viewpoint. Humans don't live that long so therefore the author of the Kings List was either wrong or it was a work of fiction. It never occurred to them that they might be missing some information. The Church has a portion of the blame here as well by not preaching about Lucifer's rule here and all that implies. The Church also took up an equally impossible timeline that Earth has only existed since Adam was created 6,000 years ago. Both sides were missing key information.

I might add that the Churches almost total lack of understanding of Ezekiel 28:2-18; Jeremiah 4:23-28 and Isaiah 14:13-14 about Lucifer's rule here on Earth led to many misinterpretations of archeological and scientific evidence. In the 1800s when Archaeology began discovering these nuggets of truth from our past they had no Biblical reference about that ancient civilization. Because the Church was not teaching about Lucifer's reign there was no knowledge of what took place here. That opened the door for the archeologists and scientists and writers to speculate about UFOs and Evolution as the answer to their question, 'What in the world happened here?' The scriptures about Lucifer's reign here on Earth answer that question and tell us about his accomplishments here and his massive failure to do what God had sent him here to do.

If the Church had been teaching on this the archeologists would have known about a civilization before Adam, Lucifer's rebellion and defeat and the first flood along with its catastrophic outcome. They would have known that the destruction was so complete God had to rebuild and recreate a lot of things in the Genesis story. And without this Biblical point of view the archeologist and experts of our day are finding many things that they can't explain so they just guess and make errors in those guesses. What if Erich von Daniken had this information in 1968? His book *Chariots of the Gods* could have told about Lucifer's civilization and the advanced technology that came to Earth through the angels. He could have answered so many more questions that have remained unsolved up to date.

Perhaps Erich von Daniken wasn't aware or familiar with the following scripture in Ezekiel. If he had known, he might have recognized that Ezekiel's description of Cherubim angels mimics the statues carved by

Indian craftsmen many thousands of years ago. First, we have to see what a Cherubim, just one species of angel, looks like from Ezekiel description.

Ezekiel 10:20-22

This is the living creature under the God of Israel by the river Chebar, and I knew they were Cherubim. Each one had **four faces** and each one had **four wings**, and the likeness of the hands of a man was under their wings, [*each hand would have to have an arm attached to it*] And the likeness of their faces was the same as the faces which I had seen by the River Chebar, [*the OX face is described as a cherub face, the second face was the face of a man, the third the face of a lion, the fourth the face of an eagle*] their appearance and their persons. Their feet are straight with the bottoms like calves feet (so hooves Ezekiel 1:1-18) Their appearance was like burning coals, and the appearance of lamps, like fire and lightning four faces:

Note that the statues found in Indian Temples have four arms and four faces. This makes me think differently about Satan as he is a Cherub as well and we know his body was covered with all manner of precious stones and inlaid with musical instruments. But this also means he has three other faces as well.

Statue of Viswakarma who was the father of engineering and built Dwaraka

Garuda Temple is the statue of Vishnu riding Garuda

So let's recap. Cherubim angels have four wings, four arms and four different faces, each had the face of a man, the face of a bull, the face of a lion, and the face of an eagle. Here in these carvings we see the artists depicts their gods having multiple faces on one head. Now in the past these statues were of fictional characters. But I believe in the truth of scripture and Ezekiel tells us that angels can have four faces and multiple arms. Since God has shown us through nature that He loves color and variety I have no problem in believing He made the angels in a variety of skin colors and many different shapes or types. And I believe that Lucifer's group of followers promoted themselves as gods in order to control the Earth's population of that time period.

The Vedas chronicles many of their activities. Lucifer and his followers had heavenly knowledge of the lower secrets of heaven, advanced technology and knowledge of magic, spells, potions, metallurgy, construction, herbs and their uses as well as many other things that were totally unknown to the humans on Earth. We see multiple arms and heads in these carvings and this is Kali. She had multiple arms and blue skin color and of course she was a female and a fierce warrior. Now in the past it has been taught that there are no female angels but scripture doesn't agree. Zechariah 5:9 tells us about two female angels.

Image of the goddess Kali depicted in New World Encyclopedia

Also there are many different types of angels depicted as you can see in these carvings.

Sumerian God Enki

Sumerian God Anunnaki

Here you see Gilgamesh holding a lion. This depiction demonstrates the size of Gilgamesh. The image beside him is a warrior of the same size only with a calves face with horns and hooves, but human body. Now since Gilgamesh is recorded as an angel and human offspring. Please remember that the Bible's description of Cherubim angels tells us they had four different faces, human, eagle, calf and lion. I feel it only reasonable to assume their offspring would have one of these face types.

The above pictures show the same Sumerian god, but as you can see he's depicted with two different faces. One of a man and the other of an eagle. Both carvings depict him as having four wings. You see below another relief carving of Gilgamesh, a king of Sumeria and an offspring of a mating between one of these angels and a human female. He's holding a full grown lion under his arm to try and give some scale of his size. The being standing beside him has the face of an ox with horns and ears plus he has hooves for feet. Sounds just like Ezekiel's description?

Varaha is a god depicted with the face of a Boar and has four arms. Narasimha is a god depicted with a Lion face and both with four arms.

Varaha Hoysaleswara Temple

Narasimha Picture found in Wikipedia

Let's look at some more of the evidence carved in stone depicting (as well as the carvers could) some of the Demi gods they were worshipping. Please keep in mind that these are relief carvings and not statues, but one can't help but notice that each of these examples has multiple faces on one being plus multiple arms and hands. I believe that if they were statues there would have been a fourth face at the back. This is reminiscent of the descriptions of Cherubim and Seraphim angels from the Bible. Although these have no visible wings God is so creative that producing spirit beings who don't have wings is not beyond God or His capabilities or His imagination. The very example of His vast creativity is on full display in nature itself here on Earth. Combine this fact with the examples of the burning sword which keeps watch at the entrance to Eden and the living wheels within wheels that are full of eyes (Ezekiel 10:12) brings me to the conclusion that God could have and would have created a massive variety of angelic types.

This image of Ganesh is
found in multiple Temples

Found in an Indian
Hindu Temple

Hoysaleswara Temple

These are modern depictions of Brahma (a male with four heads), Saraswati (a female goddess with four arms and light skin color), and Vishnu (a male human body with blue skin and four arms). We have to remember that God loves variety and to think He would have only created one or two varieties and colors of angels is ridiculous.

I find it interesting that the Bible describes the different physical appearances of angels and researchers have ignored their striking similarities to the descriptions of the Hindu gods in the ancient Hindu text (the Verda and Rigveda). Why have they not noted the Hindu descriptions of their ancient Demigods and its similarities to the Biblical description of Cherubim and Seraphim angels? We must not forget that these angels had access to God's advanced medical and military technologies.

For example there is a story of a warrior queen named Vishpala who lost her leg during a battle. The twin gods Ashwins then medically fitted her with an iron prosthetic leg which allowed her to get back to the battle. I would also assume they had very strong pain killers. Think about the imagination it would have taken to think up this story back then. A story that included an iron prosthetic leg in that day and age was impressive. However I think these texts are depicting a time in the much more distant past when the people had

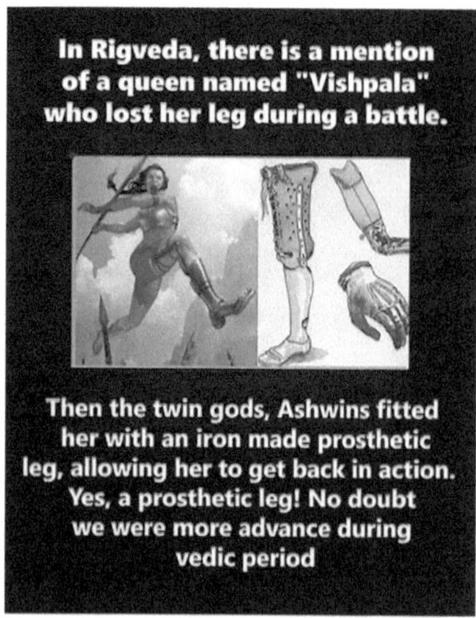

access to advanced technology as well as angels who were obviously skilled medical people. For this reason and others that I'll show you I feel these stories are chronicling Lucifer's rule on Earth and his angels' interaction with the humans of that time. Now for many reasons I believe these humans didn't have a spirit being. They were exactly like Adam before God breathed His spirit into him. They were like the animal population with a body and an intelligent brain but no spirit. These were not eternal beings as we are.

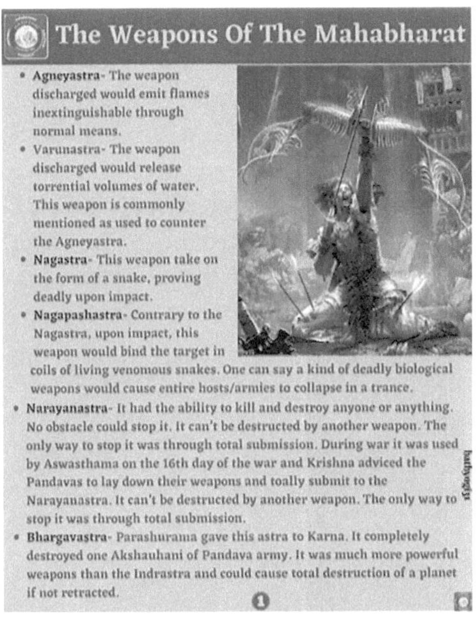

The Weapons Of The Mahabharat

- **Agneyastra**- The weapon discharged would emit flames inextinguishable through normal means.
- **Varunastra**- The weapon discharged would release torrential volumes of water. This weapon is commonly mentioned as used to counter the Agneyastra.
- **Nagastra**- This weapon take on the form of a snake, proving deadly upon impact.
- **Nagapashastra**- Contrary to the Nagastra, upon impact, this weapon would bind the target in coils of living venomous snakes. One can say a kind of deadly biological weapons would cause entire hosts/armies to collapse in a trance.
- **Narayanastra**- It had the ability to kill and destroy anyone or anything. No obstacle could stop it. It can't be destructed by another weapon. The only way to stop it was through total submission. During war it was used by Aswasthama on the 16th day of the war and Krishna adviced the Pandavas to lay down their weapons and toally submit to the Narayanastra. It can't be destructed by another weapon. The only way to stop it was through total submission.
- **Bhargavastra**- Parashurama gave this astra to Karna. It completely destroyed one Akshauhani of Pandava army. It was much more powerful weapons than the Indrastra and could cause total destruction of a planet if not retracted.

Now the Mahabharat and the Ramayana TM are two ancient Sanskrit text that tell the story of two epics in ancient India. These describe two wars between rulers during that time period and below we see a small list of some of the more exotic weapons talked about and their functions.

As you can see, the Brahma Astra weapon was not only written about, but carved in objects as well. In this case, the image here was carved onto a cylindrical seal found in Babylon. To me, the carved image in the Babylon Cylindrical metal seal is mind-

boggling. It very much resembles an Atomic bomb, but who would have had one of these many thousands of years ago? Or for that matter, how could they have described it so accurately in this story and on the metal steal of Babylon? Then again, if the carver didn't see one function, then who explained to him what to carve into the seal?

The question on our minds is, or should be, 'Are ancient stories that were written down thousands of years ago from oral traditions reliable sources of facts?' Let's take a look at one more example. This four tusk elephant, also known as Gomphotheres, was unknown to fossil hunters until 1947 when a Dutch zoologist, Heekeren, found a skeleton of this animal. According to experts this creature roamed Earth 2.6 million years ago. It is curious however that this animal is described in the Ramayana epic as guarding the Palace gates of Ravan. So before the skeletal discovery in 1947 the ancient text of Ramayana was thought to be a work of fiction. However there are many places described in the Ramayana that have been proven to be real along with all the astronomical events, which it also describes and have been confirmed by NASA.

This brings up the question, 'How accurate is the dating system the Intellectual Elites use?' I say this because of a recent New Mexico discovery. Apparently the Clovis people in the El Findel Mundo archeological site in Mexico dined on one of these beasts just 13,000 to 13,500 years ago. Now that's quite a differential spread from extinction 1.2 million years to being eaten 13,500 years ago. Other finds tell us that this animal ranged throughout North and South America. So now the question becomes, 'If this animal died out 1.2 million years ago according to the Intellectual Elites how old is the story of Ramayana?' Well the New Mexico find shows us just how inaccurate these experts guesses can be. I feel this could be helping to narrow down the time period of when Lucifer had his kingdom here on Earth for 241,000 years.

I find this encouraging. In this chapter we've learned that Lucifer's rule here on Earth was somewhat chronicled in two separate countries, India and Sumeria. The Sumerian Kings List gives us a rough timeframe seeing it ended in a catastrophic flood event. In Indian epics the experts have been able to confirm city location through archeology and astronomical events that are listed through the NASA computer. Now if we speculate that the Younger Dryas event which occurred roughly 11,800 years ago may have been the end of Lucifer's Forgotten Civilization it helps us develop a potential timeline. I like the way both cultures documented their gods in stone reliefs and statues. Although we can't date the stone of the carvings or Temples we do know from the Biblical depictions they resemble angels remarkably well. The stone ruins of megalithic structures we looked at in Chapter 5 from all over the world also seem to confirm an ancient world wide civilization was here on Earth.

CHAPTER 8

When Giants Walked the Earth

This is perhaps the chapter that shows Satan's repetitive behavior patterns. The giants were the offspring of angels when they mated with human females.

Genesis 6:1 And it came to pass, when men began to multiply on the face of the Earth, and daughters were born unto them, 2 That the sons of God saw the daughters of men that they were fair; and they took them wives of all which they chose. 3 And the Lord said, My spirit shall not always strive with man, for that he also is flesh: yet his days shall be an hundred and twenty years. 4 There were giants in the Earth in those days; and also after that, when the sons of God (fallen angels) came in unto the daughters of men, and they bare children to them, the same became mighty men which were of old, men of renown. 5 And God saw that the wickedness of man was great in the Earth, and that every imagination of the thoughts of his heart was only evil continually.

Amos 2:**9** Yet destroyed I the Amorite before them, whose height was like the height of the cedars, and he was strong as the oaks; yet I destroyed his fruit from above, and his roots from beneath.

Numbers 13: **32** And they brought up an evil report of the land which they had searched unto the children of Israel, saying, The land, through which we have gone to search it, is a land that eateth up the inhabitants thereof; and all the people that we saw in it are men of a great stature. **33** And there we saw the giants, the sons of Anak, which come of the giants: and we were in our own sight as grasshoppers, and so we were in their sight.

The iron pillar of Delhi is a structure 7.21 meters (23 feet 8 inches) high. It is corrosion resistance to this day. Scientists feel it is the result of an even layer of crystalline iron hydrogen phosphate hydrate forming on the high phosphorus content iron. This serves to protect it from the effects of the Delhi climate. The ancient writing is preserved well because of the corrosion-resistance. The experts say this pillar was built around 390 A.D. Because this iron pillar has been exposed to the elements for 1633 years and shows very little sign of weathering, it indicates to me a fallen angel revealed some metallurgy secrets to the builder at that time. We have to remember the fallen angels still interact with humans even today.

This behavior described above also happened before Adam when Lucifer reigned the Earth and after Adam's fall (when Satan again ruled the Earth) but before Noah. After Noah's flood Satan and his fallen angels were mating with females again. Joshua fought the Amorites for the Promised Land and they were a race of giants who had conquered that area. They controlled a vast number of fortified cities and the people therein. One of the giants who was named OG in the area of Bashan controlled 60 fortified cities alone. These were cruel and vicious giant warriors who ruled the conquered inhabitants without mercy and as Moses' spies observed they even ate some of those inhabitants of that land. God had Joshua and the Israelite army wipe this vicious race of giants (the Amorites) out. The mating with the females was being done to try and destroy the pure bloodline of Adam's seed (Jesus, Genesis 3:15).

To give you some idea of the size of the Amorite giants their king Og had a bed with the following dimensions of 13.5 feet long and 6 feet wide (Deuteronomy 3:11). It was made out of iron. We also have to keep in mind that Joshua lived in the latter part of the Bronze Age so for Og to have a bed made of iron he and his people would have had to been taught how to forge and temper iron hundreds of years before the iron age. This is a good example of fallen angels sharing knowledge with humans and their offspring as The Book of Enoch tells us they did. The fallen angels did not stop this practice of sleeping with human females and sharing forbidden knowledge. Take the Philistines as another example. They had Goliath and his 4 giant brothers as their champions (2 Samuel 21:15-22) who carried iron tipped spears (1 Samuel 17:4-7) and a sword made out of iron (1 Samuel 21:9, 22:10). The Philistines would not allow an Israelite to work as a blacksmith in case they learned how to forge iron weapons (1 Samuel 13:19) We can assume therefore that the fallen angels, perhaps Goliath's father, taught the Philistines how to forge weapons out of iron and they weren't taking any chances the Israelites would learn how to do this because this art was not common knowledge.

Replica of the Antikythera Device
The Antikythera Device from the 2nd century BC. The hunk of aluminum dated at 40,000 years old found in Transylvania Romania beside the bones of a woolly Mammoth and the metal sledgehammer dated at 140 million years found near London

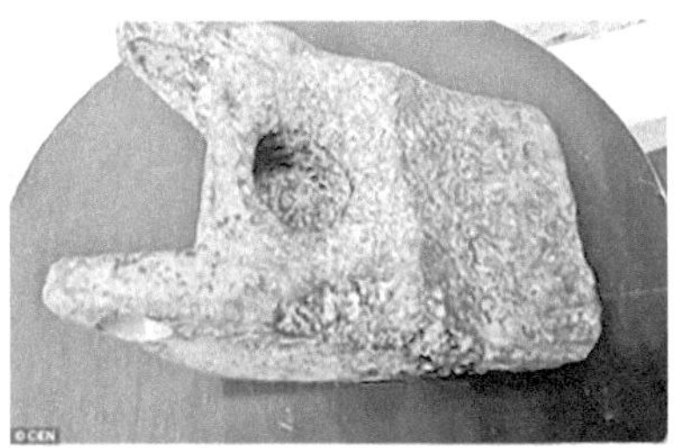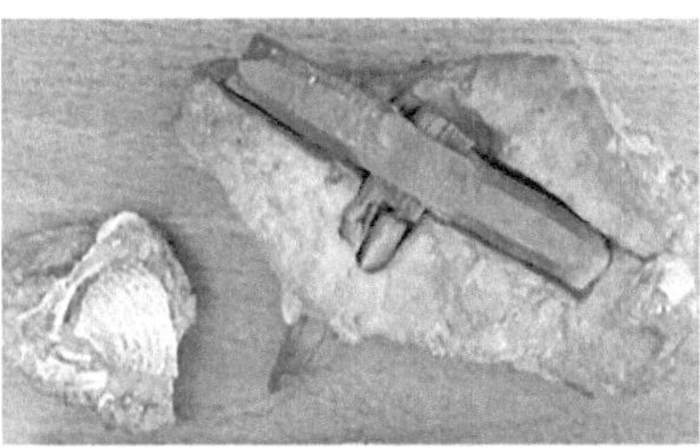

Now do you see that the fallen angels are still having input into mankind's understanding of hidden secrets? This knowledge helps us to reinterpret out of place and time artifacts that have surfaced in the past.

(Remember, we discussed these items in Chapter 4: Something Happened Here) Artifacts that should not exist in the time periods that the scientists have allocated for each one. There is no way any of these would exist without the help of an advanced intelligence that was sharing information with the Earth's population. And common sense in light of what we've studied up to this point in the book screams Fallen Angels did the sharing. Now let's have a look at some of the evidence that giants walked this Earth at some point in our past.

Facts do not cease to exist just because they have been ignored by Main Street Archeology, Science, Professors, Museums, Media and the Intellectual Elite. Although this hiding of facts has gone on for centuries the facts are still there and waiting to be rightfully interpreted with fresh eyes and open minds. Minds that use Logic, Common Sense and examine previously discounted information to reinterpret the evidence, which has always existed. Well except for the evidence that the Intellectual Elites have had the opportunity to hide or destroy in the past, according to many researchers including Xaviant Haze, author of the book *Ancient Giants*.

This is Robert Schoch standing in front of the giant footprint in granite stone near Empuluzi, South Africa

For example we have been told over and over again that giants are a figment of our imaginations. The Intellectual Elites say the Bible is a work of fiction and one of their proofs is they say giants never really existed. Well I'm sorry to burst their fictional truth bubble, but how do they explain this giant footprint in granite stone, which scientists say is 30 million years old? Or the giant 47 inch human Femur bone found in south-east Turkey in the 1950s and fortunately it was so well documented that it still exists and we have this photo of it to show you. As with so much of the evidence corroborating

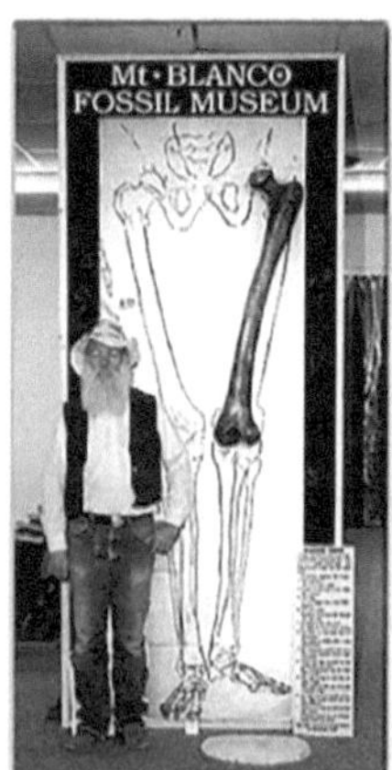

47 inch Human Femur

In the late 1950s, during road construction in south-east Turkey in the Euphrates Valley, many tombs containing the remains of Giants were uncovered. At two sites the leg bones were measured to be about 120 cms '47.24 inches'. Joe Taylor, Director of the Mt. BLANCO FOSSIL MUSEUM in Crosbyton, Texas, was commissioned to sculpt this anatomically correct, and to scale, human femur. This "Giant" stood some 14-16 feet tall, and had 20-22 inch long feet. His or Her finger tips, with arms to their sides, would be about 6 feet above the ground. The Biblical record, in Deuteronomy 3:11 states that the Iron Bed of Og, King of Bashan was 9 cubits by 4 cubits or approximately 14 feet long by 6 feet wide!

GENESIS 6:4 ———
There were Nephilim (Giants) in the earth in those days; and also after that when the sons of God (Angels?) came in unto the daughters of men, and they bare children to them, the same became mighty men which were of old, men of renown.

More info & Replicas available at mtblanco1@aol.com or www.mtblanco.com
Mt. Blanco Fossil Museum • P.O. Box 559, Crosbyton, TX 79322 • 1-800-367-7454

the existence of giants the Smithsonian or government officials took it for further study and then conveniently misplaced all these materials. An unfortunate accident or an extremely convenient one? Well, all I have to say is that they seem to be very accident prone in this regard, and Xaviant Haze agrees with this conclusion.

Another fact I did not know until this research is that the Smithsonian is not a government owned or financed institution. It is privately owned and funded by individuals not associated with any government and therefore do not have to worry about government regulations or oversight. Interesting? Now the interesting thing about searching for photographic confirmable evidence for giants has become more difficult in recent years. The internet seems to have been scrubbed clean of the legitimate photos and replaced with provable frauds. Go figure! This being the case I'm going to rely on your common sense. Very much like I did in chapter 7 on Hidden Angels. I have very little photographic evidence that hasn't been tampered with and in this case there are no statues that I can show you either.

The good thing about the Bible is that it's true whether or not you believe in it. Now the Bible, in Genesis chapter 6, tells us that giants were the offspring of fallen angels mating with human females. Since the Intellectual Elites don't want us to believe the Bible they work to discredit any discovery anywhere in the world that even remotely verifies the Bible. If they can't discredit it in any way, they then destroy or hide the evidence or have their media friends ignore it. The Smithsonian is exceptionally adept at these endeavors all around the world. Trying to get these finds documented and published when the newly discovered facts go against the accepted dogma can be dangerous. I mean the followers of the accepted dogma are stone cold vicious at times. Ruining lives and reputations just to protect their established dogma. The archeologist must fall inline or their reputations and jobs are systematically ruined.

Since they can't or won't try to explain these out of place artifacts and documented photographic evidence it suddenly goes missing. This approach is much like what Project Bluebook did for UFOs and we all know how that turned out with the Congressional hearings. The Congressional hearings showed that the government not only knew the fact that UFOs are real, but that they were hiding that fact from the public. As I said The Bible speaks of giants in Genesis 6 which came about from fallen angels mating with the women of that time and their offspring were giants and men of renown. What is not so well known is that these angels ruled this Earth under Lucifer thousands of years before Adam and Eve (Ezekiel 28:2-18; Jeremiah 4:23-28; Isaiah 14:12-15). These same angels ruined the world Lucifer reigned over so badly that God destroyed it all with the first flood (Jeremiah 4:23-28). When Adam disobeyed God he turned the rulership of Earth back to Satan. Then Satan and his angels employed the very same tactics they had used before by teaching the humans all manner of sin and mating with the females. Their unions with the women produced giants and men of renown. After a period of time, roughly 1600 years, God's response to their activities was another flood, that being Noah's flood (Genesis 6 through chapter 8). Each time God said the people had gotten to the point where they only knew how to sin (Jeremiah 4:22; Genesis 6:5-7).

The Evolutionists and Scientists say 'hog wash, impossible and there is no evidence of giants'. However there is evidence from public newspaper articles, photographs and bones which were displayed in private collections. But because the Smithsonian Institute has methodically gone around the world and tried to collect these specimens 'for further study' this evidence is no longer available. The Smithsonian seems to have a severe security problem, because none of these specimens have ever been reported on nor seen again. .We'll see how long they can keep this charade going. Here's just one account of their treachery.

In 1917 Florida the State Geologist E. H. Sellards and Professor Oliver P. Hay studied a fossil find at Vero Beach. These men were positive that their research and the evidence found at the site proved that giant human beings inhabited North America during the Pleistocene period some 2.58 million years ago. They had unearthed human bones intermingled with bones of Mastodons, saber-toothed tiger, and many other extinct animals that formerly ranged in this hemisphere. The deposit was found near Vero Beach, Florida. That the humans were of enormous size is evidenced by the bones found at the excavation. It was thought that some were ten or twelve feet in height. Some excellent specimens of the skeletons of these gigantic men have been found, some of them locked in the deadly embrace of great animals, with strange weapons of bone clutched in skeleton hands were a foot long. (Reported by Smyrna Daily News, Jan. 5/1917)

Unfortunately Sellard's and Hay's reward for this discovery and all their hard work recording it was that they were forced out of their positions and relocated far away from Florida. However the truth came out 90 years later. When at the same Vero Beach excavation an amateur fossil hunter found a carved Mastodon bone, which scientists claimed, after three years of testing as, 'the oldest, most spectacular and rare work of art in the Americas.' Not surprisingly there was no mention of the giant skeletons discovered by Sellards and Hays in the same Earth strata, which were conveniently lost shortly after arriving at the Smithsonian in 1945.

Skeletal proof that giants once roamed the Earth have been found throughout North and South America, but have also been conveniently lost by the Smithsonian. (Ancient Giants of the Americas, by Xaviant Haze) The evidence clearly shows that humans in one form or another walked this Earth along with the dinosaurs and Giants also walked the Earth among them. Scripture clearly shows that Lucifer ruled nations of men (hominids) on the Earth before his rebellion and remember he was already a fallen angel when he tempted Eve in the Garden. Therefore logic says Lucifer's rule and rebellion happened well before the creation story in Genesis and that explains the time gap between Genesis 1:1 and Genesis 1:2.

In 2 Peter 3:5 God tells us that people are willingly ignorant of the creation story, the whole creation story, and it didn't all begin with Adam and Eve as we've learned from Isaiah, Ezekiel and Jeremiah. There is much more to the creation story but God did not tell the story in a linear fashion. He purposely hid the details within scripture so we would have to search all the scriptures to find the whole truth. Joshua 1:8 tells us that God wanted us to read and think about His word constantly, but very few do. Hence we are willingly ignorant of His Truth. Man's truth is Evolution even though they can't prove it, but they are very passionate about selling their truth to everyone. Evolution says that small changes in an animal's cell structures over a long period of time (millions of years) will eventually bring about species changes in all species.

Examples they tell us are fish to land animals, land animals to birds and monkeys to human beings. They claim and teach this in our schools, according to them this is how a one cell Ameba evolved into man. We, the uneducated masses according to them, are supposed to accept this theory without question. But they themselves utterly refuse to even consider the alternative of Intelligent Design. Now back to the question did men walk with dinosaurs? Keep in mind I have only given you a few examples of the evidence that is documented, there is much, much more out there. But given this knowledge so far I'd say the answer is a resounding yes and the Creationists holding onto the firm 6,000 years theory better start reassessing their position.

They have found hundreds of vastly oversized leather bound books in the Archives of Prague Castle. They are too awkwardly large to be used by humans and they are written in an unknown language. The lost language is interesting from the point of view that to lose a language from a civilization that was advanced enough to create a library of leather bound books that would mean every member of that society would have to perish. Only one event in scriptures accounts for this and that is recorded in Jeremiah 4:23-28 OKJV. No one survived God's judgment at the end of Lucifer's rebellion. If these giant books were not used by giants in the distant past than by who and for what purpose? Certainly they are of no use to humans even now they are just interesting oddities of history from our distant past.

These pictures are supposed to be from the Archives of Prague Castle, but when I looked for the authenticity of them the information has been wiped from the internet. This sounds very similar to the missing info on giants' bones. All I can say is they at least are consistent in their cover-up. But up until this study I have never heard of these books from any source. Why would our supposed experts hide this type of interesting history? Unless they don't want anything that would bolster the case for the fact that giants had a definite society and were cultured enough to write done their knowledge so it could be shared with others. But if this information got out to the general public it would bolster the truth that giants once lived on Earth in an advanced society with culture of some sort. However this information and evidence would also confirm the Bible was correct and truthful. Not just a collection of fairytales as the Intellectual Elites would have us believe.

Museums are clearly hiding things but no one is crying "Foul"?

Is there evidence that any of our modern day creatures evolved from dinosaur times? There is no evidence of evolving, but there is evidence that modern creatures lived alongside dinosaurs. Really, that's true! There is fossil evidence that these evolutionists are totally ignoring. Let's look at some. The fossil of a small rat-like mammal with well-preserved internal organs has been found in a limestone quarry in Spain. Long-age believing paleontologists say. The fossil is 125 million years old. According to their timeline this pushes back the record of well-preserved mammalian organs, fur, and skin, by more than 60 million years. Evolutionists predicted that mammals living at this time would be primitive, yet the internal organs in the fossil reveal that the mammal was just the same as mammals living today. (**Creation Magazine 38(2) 2016**) As you can see, the internal organs of supposedly 60 million year old rat are the same as modern day rats. So, where is the evolution?

Fossils found but kept secret until now, whoops!

In the vicinity of Langbaan Western Cape, South Africa, there is a Fossil Park that contains the bones of over 200 different species of animals. It has been called an animal salad, by archeologists, that contains bones of giant wild pigs, over 40 specimens of aardvarks, numerous long-necked and short necked giraffes (sivatheres), and 5 different species of hyena. Also an extinct form of hippo, a three toed horse called hipparion, 3 species of elephant, bontebok antelopes, as well as the boselaphine which today is found only in Asia, a saber-toothed cat, a wolverine, an enormous African bear, and a large number of smaller animals. Of birds there are no less than 10,000 (identified so far) bones of 90 different species, including marine birds such as cormorants, penguins, and an albatross, shorebirds, songbirds, parrots, woodpeckers, and at least one species of ostrich. Of even more importance, included in the jumble of bones are those of seals, whales and megalodon sharks, creating a mixture of marine, avian, and land mammal bones that were laid down in this single catastrophic event. **Len de Beer, Creation Magazine 38(3) 2016**

Just in case you missed it they found **10,000 bird fossils** so far and quite a large list of modern day bird species. Those bones were fossilized with the Dinosaur bones and no one is mentioning them or displaying those fossils among the dinosaur fossils and they were found beside each other. Also, no one is mentioning the fact that no evolution is involved in these bird species yet they too lived with the dinosaurs.

Dr. Carl Werner's book and DVD, Living Fossils, reveals that fossil researchers have found many modern bird remains with dinosaurs, yet museums do not display these fossils, thus keeping this information from the public. Dr. Werner visited 10 dinosaur digs and 60 museums all over the world. He interviewed various paleontologists during which he compiled a list of modern bird fossils found with dinosaur fossils. Dr. Werner discovered that many types of modern bird fossils have been found with dinosaurs including ducks, loons, flamingos, albatross, owls, penguins, sandpipers, parrots, cormorants, avocets, as well as extinct birds such as Mononykus, Archaeopleryx and Hesperornis. While these extinct birds did have teeth, there were many other modern types of birds without teeth that have been found. (So no evolution of these birds) By leaving this fact out, the museum displays mislead the public. (**Creation Magazine 34(3) 2012**)

Okay, Dr. Werner confirms what has been suspected for decades. That being the Museums, Evolutionists, Scientists, Schools and Government officials and agencies have been working together to systematically promote and teach the false narrative of Evolution. The other part of these conspirators is the News Media and the total silence that is echoing from their supposed halls of truth. Their total silence on these glaring discrepancies should be a flashing neon warning sign to every Scientist that says they believe in the truth and to every Christian. They are not hiding their efforts to conceal the proof that the Bible and your faith are real and can be proven. Stand up and start fighting back Christians. This new knowledge that Lucifer headed an ancient civilization here on Earth long before Adam blows the top right off The Theory of Evolution, so use that knowledge to your witnessing advantage.

Have they ever found the missing link?

Add to this the fact that they have been looking for a missing link for human or any animal since Darwin put forth this false theory in 1859. Their success rates for this endeavor is 100% ZERO as we have seen earlier. Also keep in mind always that the evolutionists have a very tenuous relationship with the truth. This becomes very apparent in their rush to find the elusive missing link to man and animals. Since Darwin's publication in 1859 there have been many frauds put forward as proof of this missing link.

1. Java man in the 1890s,
2. Ramapithecus Man in 1904,

3. Piltdown Man in 1912,

4. Nebraska Man in 1920, and

5. Lucie in the 1930s.

All of which have been proven to be fakes for the missing link. Yet we still see them in full color renderings in school textbooks and displayed in museums around the world as facts that men evolved from apes. There have also been numerous fakes put forward for the missing links of evolution in the animal kingdom, all eventually proved to be fake, but no retractions have ever been given.

Winston Churchill once said, "A lie can travel halfway around the world before the truth has a chance to get its pants on." I think that was right for Churchill's time, but today it only takes seconds for a lie to spread around the world on social media platforms.

CHAPTER 9

Can We Trust Ancient Stories?

I feel the answer is yes, but to a point. They should be viewed through the lens of the Bible.

KUMARI KANDAM - India

Indian ancient stories tell of a civilization on the coast in South East India that had massive libraries and Universities. The story says this city was attacked from the sky by a vehicle with strange destructive weapons and it sunk into the sea. All thought this story to be fiction until marine Archeologists found Kumari Kadam in 2002 under water at Poompuhar (Tamil Nadu). It extends more than 5km from shore down to depths of more than 30 meters.

Corala Temple - India

Legend has it, and it's holding up so far, that Vault B can only be opened by a specific incantation, but no one seems to remember it so the vault remains shut for now. They say there are ropes of gold, belts made out of diamonds and gigantic emeralds. The Temple is dedicated to Vishnu, references in Tamil writing in the 6th century but was thought to be very old even back then. Vault B is the only vault of the Temple 6 vaults that has never been opened. All the other 5 contained treasures.

Stories from India Ancient past come true

Mysuru - India, Institute

Scholars are studying the ancient Indian script Sanskrit Text - which date back to 4,000 years.

Hinduism has millions of gods of all description but the text also shows these gods traveling around in floating cities, magic stones and flying machines. Hinduism is built on that their gods arrived here from deep space. The text depicts beings with multiple arms, beings with at least three faces, cloven hooves for feet, and animal like faces. This should not surprise Christians and if it does you haven't studied the Bible. The angelic beings described in the Bible are very similarly described and they did come to Earth with Lucifer as we have seen in previous chapters.

In the Mahabharata it describes the god Krishna ruling over the kingdom of Dwarka, which was attacked and destroyed by an incredible flying machine that had highly advanced weapons. This flying craft destroyed the kingdom as it flew over. The kingdom and main city of Dwarka disappeared into the sea after the attack. In 1983 - some 4,000 years after this text was written. **Archeologist Dr. S. R. Rao** using modern sea exploration equipment began finding many artifacts under the sea. The undersea archeology was being done in the exact location where the city of Dwarka was supposed to have existed on the westernmost coast of India in the modern-day Gujarat. Indian archeologists for years had thought this was a myth, but when these artifacts began to be discovered they realized they had found the submerged ruins of Dwarka. Conclusion is that at least this part of the Mahabharata is accurate.

Another ancient Sanskrit story tells that a great deluge was sent by the god Inda to destroy the 7 Pagodas of Molly Bolly Puram, today one stands on its own. However on December 26, 2004 a massive tsunami caused the water to temporarily drop and expose a number of mysterious formations along the shoreline. Upon closer examination they were found to be man-made structures and were discovered to be the ruins of the lost Pagodas of Molly Bolly Puram. These Pagodas were said to have been destroyed in an attack from the air. This after scholars, Archeologists, learned men all for thousands of years had said this story was just a myth. These recent discoveries seem to prove that the Sanskrit text really are historical accounts. Graham Hancock reported on this find saying this civilization predates the Egyptian and Sumerians by thousands of years.

Warengal India - Fortress

The base of the structure is comprised of massive granite blocks, no mortar was used to hold them together. The stones were cut, carved and polished using a method and technique they don't understand today. Similar structure to the ones found in South America.

Plato wrote about the destruction of the great civilization of Atlantis, a culture that developed advanced technology but grew large and poor in character, and were punished for it. Atlantis was done in by its own hubris. That is because of the progress, because of the achievements, because of the genius that was Atlantis, arrogance started sneaking in. They started to use their great military power to conquer neighbors, just for the sake of domination. They started to take their magic for granted and used it without moral reasoning. The story goes that Poseidon became concerned with their arrogance so he brought earthquake and floods and Atlantis was swallowed up. (This would definitely fit right into the scriptures describing Lucifer and his reign on Earth before Adam)

When Herodotus visited Egypt around 450 BC, he described the construction of an unusual river boat on the Nile, called a Baris, with long internal ribs. For centuries, scholars have argued over his account because there was no archaeological evidence that such ships ever existed. That is until 2019. A fabulously preserved example of about 70% of the hull of a Baris has been located in the sunken Egyptian port city of Thons-Heracleion. "It wasn't until we discovered this wreck that we realized Herodotus was right," said Dr. Damian Robinson, director of Oxford University's center for maritime archaeology. (**Creation Magazine 42(1) 2020**)

Herodotus has been proven right before this. His account of encountering a race of warrior women which he named the Amazons, when he travelled north of the Black Sea in around 450 BC. Herodotus also claimed that there were large, furry ants that enriched the Persian Empire by burrowing for gold. They were bigger than foxes, but smaller than dogs. Some recent discoveries suggest, perhaps surprisingly, that both accounts are based on solid truth. An American archaeologist, referring to burial mounds in central Asia associated with cultures dated from 600 to 200 BC, says that about one in six of the graves of women contain the sort of weaponry normally associated with a warrior's grave. The weapons, which had clearly been used, had handgrips smaller than men's weapons.

What about the 'gold-digging ants'? A French explorer and a British photographer believe that Herodotus is totally vindicated. They have discovered marmots, cat-sized rodents, burrowing in a shallow stratum of gold bearing sandy soil on Pakistan's Dansar Plain. The confusion likely came about because the ancient Persian word for marmot means 'mountain ant'. Although only recently able to visit the military sensitive area, Michel Peissel first heard about them in 1983.

Local tribesmen told him that their ancestors extracted gold from the sand by using the marmots to burrow into the sand. Then when the marmots came back to the surface the gold was stuck to the animal's fur and was then deposited on the surface.

1. **Holmes, B., 1997, Women warriors come back from the grave. New Scientist, 153 (2068):17**

2. **Sancton, T. 1996, Golden "ants" Time, December 9, 1996, p.70. creation.com/golden-ants**

The evidence shows how the Intellectual Elites are hiding things and information from the general public. They are making huge errors in time estimates and ignoring evidence proving the Truth of the Bible. As we have seen there are clearly errors in the estimates of elapsed time and there is a case to be made for two catastrophic flood events plus evidence of men before Adam. Both the Evolutionists and the Creationists have to recalibrate their time elapsed estimates so there is room for debate as well as proper investigation and study. A study by Scientists which will keep an open mind as to which of these arguments best fits the evidence.

This complex reminds me of a very large and elaborate ant nest. It is 280 feet deep with 15,000 little ventilation shafts, which bring fresh air to the deepest areas. The whole complex is built over an underground river that was probably used as its water source. It is an underground city that is thousands of years old. So old in fact that no one knows who built it and for that matter no one even knew it existed until its accidental discovery in 1963. There is an ancient legend that the god Enki warned the people of Cappadocia to build this in order to survive a coming Ice Age. I'd say they believed him because there have been found 200 multi-level underground complexes throughout Cappadocia. Some of which are connected to each other by underground tunnels. This one in Derinkuyu would have held 20,000 men, women and children in rock rooms. There are 13 stories in this complex, which also had religious centers, store rooms, wine presses and stables for livestock. It has huge round boulders which were carved to roll into place and block the entrance tunnels. **This would have been impossible to build with stone hammers and chisels not to mention the advanced engineering and planning that would have been involved.**

Now we have to tie some of this archeological evidence together here. I say this because the archeologists seem to be studying these finds in Turkey as if they had no connection to one another. I don't believe that to be true. Remember the other finds we discussed in Chapter 5 of Mega Construction around the world? Gobekli-Tepe and a second site they named Karahan-Tepe. Both in Turkey and now we add to that puzzle these 200 underground complexes in Cappadocia Turkey. We have to be aware that scientists can't date rock, but I believe all of this construction was built around the same time period. The dating that archeologists came up with for Gobekli-Tepe was around 12,500 years in age and remember Gobekli-Tepe and Karahan-Tepe were buried intentionally under sand. Is it possible that the fallen angel Enki knew about the coming Younger Dryas Event and had them bury Gobekli-Tepe and Karahan-Tepe to preserve those sites? Then help the people in Cappadocia dig the 200 underground complexes in the hope that some of them might survive the coming Ice Age? Now we should note here that scientists tell us that the Younger Dryas Event was followed by a mini Ice Age that had a quick and severe drop in temperature to begin with.

These preceding ancient stories and archeological evidence indicate that something happened here on Earth and it happened before Adam. So let's take a look at a possible timeline. In my opinion the argument for

Creation vs Evolution have taken two opposite but equally rigid positions regarding the time frames involved. The Evolutionists say 20 million to billions of years and the Creationists rigidly hold to 6,000 years and no more. Some Christians, not all, refuse to budge while they try to fit all geological, archeological and scientific discoveries into the 6,000 year timeline. But the Creationists are ignoring Ezekiel, Isaiah, Jeremiah, Matthew, Mark and Revelation. For those who maintain they believe in the whole word of God they are certainly leaving out significant portions of scripture along with vast amounts of archeological, fossil and scientific evidence that don't fit their timeline. The above scriptures speak of Lucifer before his rebellion, the world he ruled over with men and animals as well as the events that surrounded the catastrophic flood that followed Lucifer's defeat.

When one is trying to understand anything including scripture and an archeological find no evidence, artifact or theory should be discarded or excluded until it is disproved. Now Graham Hancock said, 'Egyptologists find facts to fit their theories when they should be forming theories based on the facts.' And I agree, but it is not just Egyptologists who are doing this - it is happening worldwide. Evidence is found then judged as too whether or not it fits the accepted dogma and then it is broadcast to the world if it fits and hidden or destroyed if it doesn't fit. This is not just happening in the secular world but also within the church and that is a problem for both sides of this argument. A good example of this is the age of the Sphinx. Now Christians that want to believe everything started 6000 years **B**efore **P**resent with Adam don't care how old the Sphinx is proven to be. However, they most definitely should because it's actually exposing part of the truth of Lucifer's rule here on Earth in the distant past. And it exposes the attempted cover up by the World's Intellectual Elites to hide any evidence that the Bible is true. The Egyptologists are trying to maintain their reputations and positions as the experts on where civilization began and how long it's been here.

Their theory of wind and sand erosion has been replaced with the fact that it has been proven that the Sphinx erosion was caused by water and specifically heavy rains. This new fact is one that was known before but discarded because it didn't fit the accepted dogma of wind and sand erosion. However water erosion challenges the accepted dogma of the Sphinx being constructed in 2500 BC. The problem now is that this type of rainfall hasn't been present in Egypt for more than 5000 years according to the climatic history of the Eastern Sahara. It makes their claim of the Sphinx construction date being 2500 BC irrelevant.

The excavation history of the Sphinx comes into play here, so let's have a look at it. It is an enormous size of 66 feet tall and 240 feet long and carved out of a solid limestone rock and unfortunately scientists cannot date rock. Also, there is no contemporary text or hieroglyphs that mention the construction of the Sphinx and it should have been documented if it was built in 2500 BC. Whenever it was built it was an extraordinary feat, because it was carved out of one huge solid limestone rock. They began by cutting out blocks of limestone which weighed 50 to 200 tons and these were lifted out and transported to two different building sites to construct the Sphinx Temple and the Valley Temple. Both of which are huge complexes and both were turned to rubble in the cataclysmic flood following Lucifer's defeat. The Intellectual Elites of the world Sciences totally ignore the Bible's account of Lucifer's advanced civilization here on Earth which existed for at least 265,510 years (according to the Sumerian Kings List) at some point during our distant past.

Archeologists maintain they know how civilization developed and it was only 10,000 years ago when humans started to crawl out of caves and form communities. So for them to acknowledge the Biblical facts they would have to reassess all their theories and dogma. And for reasons known only to them they are not willing to do this. However when they found Gobekli

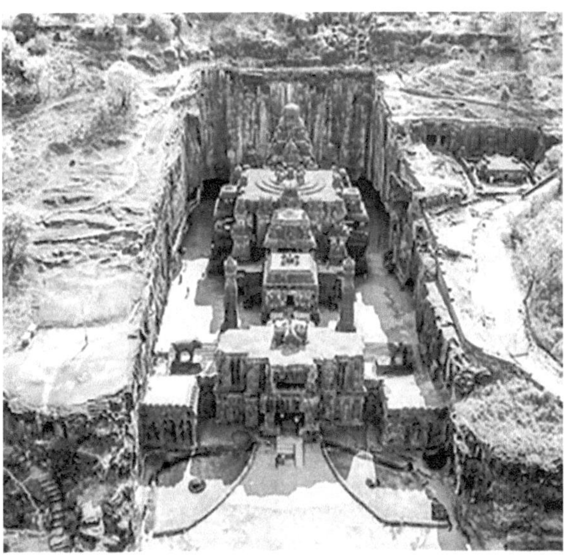

Kailosa Temple, Ellora

Tepe in Turkey they had no choice but to reassess their timeline as it was proven to have been built at least 14,500 years **Before Present**. So the Elites have been proven wrong before this and I might add many times. Anyway along with the destruction of these temples there is evidence of many pyramids throughout Egypt that were turned to rubble as well and very few people talk about these. Also, the Sphinx is not unique to this type of construction because there is a temple in India which was also carved out of a solid rock.

Now because of the evidence of water erosion there is a possible timeline that might explain at least part of the mystery and that is the Younger Dryas event at the end of the last Ice Age roughly 14,500 **BP**. This event was worldwide and the evidence for it is a black line of deposits which exists in the strata levels of the Earth worldwide. It was caused by a huge solar storm of humongous proportions and scientists say it melted huge volumes of ice producing cataclysmic runoffs of water. The last Ice Age began 2.6 million years ago and started to end 11,700 years ago, and the Laurentide Ice sheet stretched from the Arctic down to New York and was up to 3 kilometers thick in areas. When the Younger Dryas solar event triggered an age-ending melt, it is estimated that 9000 cubic kilometers of water were added to the oceans. Now this information adds more to our understanding, as to when Lucifer reigned here on Earth, which probably was around 300,000 years before the Younger Dryas event. Definitely long before Adam.

Since it has been geologically confirmed that the Younger Dryas event occurred around 14,500 years BP we have a probable date for the Cataclysmic event of Jeremiah 4:23-28. Therefore the Sphinx had to have been already carved and existed for many thousands of years before in a rain drenched environment in order to achieve the water erosion it is displaying. Also, please remember that Gobekli Tepe has been archaeologically confirmed to be 12,000 years old, so it too was constructed and buried in sand long before this event took place. But who carved it because our scientists and archeologists have always maintained that humans living back then were hunter gatherers living in caves and using rock hammers and chisels. Frankly for those tools to be used to produce 50 to 200 ton stones that were used in the construction of the aforementioned temples in those size of structures is just simply ridiculous to imagine. No there had to have been a sophisticated and very advanced civilization back when the Sphinx was carved out of the solid limestone rock to accomplish these feats of engineering.

The age of the Sahara Desert has come into question and the Elite experts have always maintained that it is millions of years old. But in 2014 the desert was studied extensively by scientists from Norway, France and China and the tests showed it was only a few thousand years old. Plus they showed it was once rich in vegetation growth akin to the Amazon Rain Forest with an abundant population of people and animals. The Sahara Desert covers an area larger than the entire USA and stretches from Egypt to the Atlantic African coast. The study showed that it took as little as 100 to 500 years to transform this vast area into the current desert. It's been estimated to have occurred anywhere from 5000 to 11000 years BP.

The 11000 year period is interesting because it falls again around the Younger Dryas event. Old legends tell us that the Nile River use to also have a tributary at its bottom that ran west to east. Herodotus wrote about this in 425 BC and said that it originated in the Mauritanian Desert which was verified in 2015. Using Satellite imaging, drones and ground penetrating radar they have found there were three different networks of rivers all dating to roughly around 5000 years ago. Also they found the beds of 5 very large fresh water lakes along this water system. The largest of these lakes was called Lake Chad and covered over 139,000 square miles of Central Africa. To put it into perspective the Great Lakes of North America when combined only take up 94,250 square miles. It is said these lakes in the Sahara all dried up about 5000 years ago. These new discoveries imply that the Sahara Desert was once a paradise up to possibly 5000 years ago.

Therefore, the next question that arises is what the Sahara Desert was like before 9700 years ago. With the advent of technological advances in drones and satellite technology along with ground penetrating radar they are finding many things they didn't know about before and this tech has been dubbed as Archeology from Space. Remember that when the Egyptian monuments and structures were discovered in the early 1800s they were buried in sand. Also remember that Gobekli Tepe's 300 acre complex was buried under hundreds of feet of sand when it was discovered, plus the Bosnian Pyramids were also buried in Earth to the point that people living beside them just thought they were three oddly shaped mountains until the Earth was removed.

There is something else to consider and that is the modern Egyptian language has no resemblance to the ancient hieroglyphics and if not for the Rosette Stone they may still not understand them. Then we have to speculate on what kind of cataclysmic event had the power to destroy some of the Pyramids and topple many of the huge statues and all the Mega cities of the ancient world. Well the Biblical scriptures say it was the cataclysmic flood that God sent upon the world after Lucifer's rebellion was defeated Jeremiah 4:23-28. Scriptures say every city and even some mountains were destroyed in that first flood. So that means thousands upon thousands of years separate Lucifer's ancient and advanced civilization from our modern one. We need to really use our imaginations to understand what that civilization was like. We can get hints and glimmers of insight from the ancient stories and the evidence of the remaining ruins.

Then we have the 900 Easter Island statues which appeared to be just carved heads. That is until someone started to dig around one and found it extended 30 feet down in the sediment. It is felt by many that this all proves extreme age but I also feel it proves there were two floods as well. Why would a society spend their time doing this?

For a moment just imagine the day when Lucifer and his fellow angels arrived on Earth probably around 300,000 years before Adam. (Remember these are some of the 8 different Hominids that existed before Adam at some point in Earth's past according to Zoology) The inhabitants here would have been very primitive and going about their daily business under a clear blue sky. Suddenly the sky was filled with flying ships of all sizes and description. Imagine the perspective from Earth when the clear blue skies above suddenly began to fill with strange floating objects some of which were as immense as mountains. They seem to be popping out of the sky itself until the whole horizon was filled with them. The humans (hominids) would have scattered in fear, but after a while they began to emerge from hiding to stare in wonder at the strange floating objects.

Eventually when the crowd was large enough one ship broke from the others and landed on the Earth and contact was made. According to the ancient Hindu stories called the Veda and the Mahabharatha these crafts where God's advanced technology which were used to bring Lucifer and his crew of angels to the Earth. This technology was necessary to accomplish the task which God had assigned to them. The task was to start an organized civilization on Earth and develop it to the point where someday the angels could leave and that new civilization would continue on its own and thrive. The Veda is one account of things that may have happened in India but Lucifer's angels were spread out worldwide in all regions of the Earth. However in India the Veda describes that after a period of time a human by the name of Ajuna was taught by them and he learned so well that he became a liaison between the human workforce and the angels in charge of that area of the world.

The Veda tells how Ajuna was taken regularly in one of the smaller flying ships to meet with the angels who were guiding specific projects. Ajuna even had his own regular driver for these journeys and his name was Malali. This craft took him up to one of the 5 floating cities where the angels lived and I assume they lived here because of the primitive living conditions existing on the Earth at that moment in time. While there Ajuna witnessed hundreds upon hundreds of smaller flying craft moving around these floating cities. Ajuna called them Vimana but there were many different varieties of these smaller flying ships which he saw every time he was taken up. Now back when this was translated it would all seem like fiction. No one in the 1500s through to the late 1800s had even seen an aircraft let alone a floating city. So then how would anyone thousands of years ago even comprehend flying crafts and floating cities without seeing them? But they would have done their best to try and describe them to others through their stories.

As we've discussed in Chapter 7 on Hidden Angels that the astronomical events described in these stories have been confirmed by NASA as having occurred. The cities and locations described have been confirmed through archeological digs and discoveries over the years. The strange animals like the four tusked elephants (although thought to be myths) have been discovered as fossilized skeletons in archeological digs all around the world. Now all this new archeological and astronomical confirmation lends a great amount of credence to the validity of these ancient stories. Oh I'm not saying they weren't exaggerated in parts, but I am saying they should not be discounted entirely.

You see only in the last 120 years have we've been to the moon, we have rockets, space station, airplanes, etc. Also there are many references in the Bible to flying machines or as the Bible likes to call them Chariots of Fire. Although the Bible has been called a work of fiction it is not and has been proven true many times. However there is the mention of 5 floating cities here in the Veda and if you read the Bible you'll see that Revelation

21-22:1-6 describes a huge floating city called New Jerusalem. Which is 1500 miles square and 1500 miles high with a base of at least 1500 miles just for balance. So I don't see why today anyone should have a problem of the concept of flying machines or floating cities. We are constantly musing about UFOs and Extraterrestrials and wondering who they are, where they came from and did they interfere with life here on Earth?

Now the question that has probably come to your mind, 'Does God have such technology as flying craft?' The short answer is yes! Lucifer and his angels would have had access to all of it when he was Covering Cherub for the Earth.

The Bible speaks of God coming to Earth and speaking with men. The vehicle He used on those occasions not only carried Him but His throne room and His entourage of angels. This vehicle was always camouflaged with clouds. The following is a description of His arrival at Mount Sinai to speak with Moses.

Moses lived 3300 years ago:

> Exodus 19: **16** Then it came to pass on the third day, in the morning, that there were thunderings and lightnings, and a thick cloud on the mountain; and the sound of the trumpet was very loud, so that all the people who *were* in the camp trembled. **17** And Moses brought the people out of the camp to meet with God, and they stood at the foot of the mountain. **18** Now Mount Sinai *was* completely in smoke, because the Lord descended upon it in fire. Its smoke ascended like the smoke of a furnace, and the whole mountain quaked greatly. **19** And when the blast of the trumpet sounded long and became louder and louder, Moses spoke, and God answered him by voice.

Did you notice the clouds cloaking the vehicle? The thunder and lightning was coming from the cloud covering and did you note the trumpet being sounded louder and louder? The trumpet was to announce the arrival of God. Wow! Remember in Chapter 6 when I described the events on the night Jesus was born? That night was also marking the Jewish New Year. An event that was always heralded by 100 Shofar Horns being blown on the city walls of Jerusalem. However, unknown to them at that time they were Trumpeting the arrival of King Jesus.

Ezekiel 1:4 describes this craft a little differently.

4 Then I looked, and behold, a whirlwind was coming out of the north, a great cloud with raging fire engulfing itself; and brightness was all around it and radiating out of its midst like the color of amber, out of the midst of the fire.

The same description of clouds used for cloaking the transport vehicle whenever God comes for a visit in the Old Testament. Ezekiel 1:22-28 adds to the description of this vehicle and its content. I'll let you read those for yourself. Now we come to King David's vision of God's chariots.

David said by inspiration that God rides on the clouds and that God's chariots numbered in the thousands of thousands, but you may not know that back in David's time they had no concept of millions or billions so for an innumerable quantity they said thousands upon thousands.

> Psalm 68:4 Sing to God, sing praises to His name;
> Extol Him who rides on the clouds,
> By His name Yah,
> And rejoice before Him.
> Psalm 68:17 The chariots of God *are* twenty thousand,
> *Even* thousands of thousands;
> The Lord is among them *as in* Sinai, in the Holy *Place.*

So I'd say it is a safe assumption that they number in the millions at least. Now we've heard about God's vehicles (chariots as the Bible calls them). But the ancient stories from India call them Vimana. I believe these were seen by Zechariah 2500 years ago.

> Zechariah 6:1 And I turned and lifted up mine eyes,
> and looked, and behold, there came four chariots out
> from between two mountains; and the mountains were
> mountains of brass.
> Zechariah 6:2 In the first chariot were red horses; and in
> the second chariot black horses;
> Zechariah 6:3 And in the third chariot white horses;
> and in the fourth chariot grisled and bay horses.

Some Bible commentators say these brass mountains are real but there is no geological record of any fully brass mountain in this area of Israel, let alone two. I have another explanation for these and it is that there was a much larger transport vehicle which was cloaked from Zechariah's sight.

Then when the loading doors were used the cloaking wasn't effective in that area of the ship and Zechariah was able to see the brass colored doors slide open for the smaller transport vehicles to leave the larger craft and bring their cargo to the Earth. The smaller craft were not cloaked. Now there probably are many varieties of these smaller transport vehicles for different purposes, but here they are transporting horses. Therefore I can imagine Ajuna being picked up in one of the Vimana as he called them and flown by his pilot Malali up to one of the 5 floating cities where the angels lived. Enoch was taken around on his adventures by a similar flying craft and he apparently had a regular driver as well (from the Book of Enoch).

Do you see now when you look at all the different ancient accounts and archeological and scientific evidence through the lens of the Bible itself you get an entirely different viewpoint on History? And if we were viewing the evidence of archeology and science through the lens of the Bible we would see there is no way to prove the world's Theories of Evolution and the Big Bang.

God has shown us in scripture that there are various stages in His creation process and none of them involve Evolution or the accidental creation of the Big Bang Theory.

The Bible has the answers to these questions and many others. Scripture tells us that the angels are inter-dimensional extraterrestrial beings. They are from a different dimension. Examples:

1. An angel brought Abraham a ram for sacrifice and appeared suddenly as if from thin air (Genesis 22)

2. Balaam's donkey seeing the angel that Balaam couldn't (Numbers 22:1-35)

3. Elisha's servant seeing God's army around the Syrian army, but the Syrians couldn't see this army (2 Kings 6:11-23)

4. Shadrach, Meshach and Abednego could be seen in the furnace but they were with an angel in a different dimension. When they came out even the smell of smoke was not on their clothing (Daniel 3:8-27)

5. Daniel was visited by an angel in the lions' den. The angel suddenly appears by entering the lions' den from the other dimension (Daniel 6)

6. God's dimension is on a different dimensional time system than ours. 2 Peter 3:8 tells us that a 1000 of our years is equal to only one of God's days. All the angels have the same dimensional time as God.

And yes, the angels are extraterrestrial beings in the sense they were not born or created here on Earth. The scriptures and the ancient stories do give us insight into what Lucifer and his angels did here on Earth when he was the Covering Cherub of Earth appointed by God (Ezekiel 28:14). Lucifer and his crew would have had access to all of these technologies and vehicles and Heavenly knowledge when they departed from Heaven to come to Earth many thousands of years ago.

We've already seen the scriptures in the Bible that layout in summary form Lucifer's reign here on Earth. So when the Vada writings talk about 5 floating cities and flying transport vehicles it doesn't cause me one little iota of hesitation. Because I've already read (many times) in the Bible that Lucifer had ruled here well before Adam and Eve. Also that God used a transport vehicle (with a cloud cloaking device) to move His throne room unseen from place to place (Exodus 19:16-19; Ezekiel 1:4). God's angels also used other smaller flying vehicles (using a larger vehicle to transport them) to shuttle horses and riders to the Earth to scout it (Zechariah 6:1-8).

So these descriptions in the ancient Indian texts ring plausible to me, because God has told us in scripture that He has this technology and Lucifer had complete access to it. These ancient writings (I feel) give us insight into how long Lucifer reigned here for over 265,510 years (A time span determined from the Sumerian Kings List). How miserable he became as a ruler and his compatriots were even worse. That they warred against each other and mistreated the humans they ruled over. Also they tell us (much like the Book of Enoch) what they taught the humans (weapons, sexual behavior, spells, potions, incantations, etc.) How the angels used the lower secrets of heaven for their advantage. That they warred against God which resulted in that world being completely destroyed in a catastrophic flood (Jeremiah 4:23-28). So by knowing this, it gives us a little more insight into God and how His dimension functions. This should make us more secure in our faith.

We know what these ancient writings say through their interpretation by experts.

The Sumerian Dynasty that preceded the first great flood (Lucifer's flood) lasted at least 265,510 years and was ruled by 8 kings with an average reign of 30,000 yrs. The narrative begins with 8 nonhuman kings (ruling angels under Lucifer) for a total of 241,000 years. During that period the records show one king ruled for 43,200 years and another named Alulim ruled in Eridug for 28,800 years according to the Sumerian Kings List. After 241,000 years the angels handed the reign of rule over to hybrid human kings, ending in a cataclysmic flood. Comparing the lifespans of the first 8 angelic rulers would be comparable to comparing a human lifespan to that of an ant. Some of the oldest Sumerian text ever discovered describe a ruler named Gilgamesh as 2/3 god and 1/3 man the result of an angel mating with a human female. He was a King of Iraq who saw everything, learned everything, understood everything, who knew everything that happened before the deluge. He traveled far and wide over land and sea. Gilgamesh was one of the transition kings, between angels and human hybrids, he was only one of 23 kings with an average reign of 1,000 years covering a period of 24,510 yrs. 3 months, 3.5 days. The Sumerians were very precise. From the Sumerian culture we got 360 degrees in a circle, 60 seconds in a minute and 60 minutes in an hour

So at this point we know from scripture that Lucifer ruled the Earth in the distant past and that was before Adam and Eve were created. He was very successful in creating mining operations, which we know were very lucrative. The Bible tells us that he obtained great wealth and was very proud of this fact. Also he obviously divided the Earth into different sectors and placed his most loyal and capable followers over those areas to develop them. Scriptures only give a high overview and summary of this time period. So how do we find out details about this distant period of time and this civilization? Well, as you've seen in Chapter 4 Something Happened Here, archeological finds have pulled back the veil of time a bit and given us glimpses as to what might have happened. The Sumerian culture also kept detailed records on clay tablets as it turns out. A total of 200,000 clay tablets from the Mesopotamian culture were unearth in the 1500s. They were archived for 300 years until 1835 when Henry Ralenson arrived in Iran to translate them.

In those tablets the earliest stories are not about God but about contact with the Anunnaki, and

Zecharia Sitchin highlighted what he thought was the truth. In his mind, contact with the Anunnaki was contact with Extraterrestrials, because the word Anunnaki equals 'those who came from the heavens to Earth.' Sitchin was right to a point they were Extraterrestrials, but he missed that they were also inter-dimensional beings, and God calls them angels. You see, at that point in time, it seems no one knew that the Bible speaks of Lucifer and one third of the angels coming to Earth and ruling it for thousands of years. If they did know, they have made it their life's work to hide that fact and any evidence that supports it.

Supposedly, the Anunnaki changed the human DNA to create human hybrids more suited to their purposes, as they needed a workforce for mining and labor. This is also confirmed in The Book of Giants which was removed from the Biblical Canon, along with the Book of Enoch and many others some 300 years after Jesus. These books contain information that the Church seems to want to keep hidden from us. However, these books are still available to us through the Orthodox Church because they didn't remove them from their Bible. They split from the mainstream Church over this as well as the changes to the calendars and other things. The Jewish Book of Mysteries also has references to the deeds of the fallen angels at that time.

Then in 1896, Nathaniel Schmidt who was a Professor of Samilitic languages at Colgate University, Hamilton, NY. For 11 yrs. he had taught here presenting subjects in different languages. He was the authority on ancient Middle Eastern text and language. His work of translation confirmed that the Sumerian account seems to parallel the Biblical account. Problem is that even though he was a Baptist minister he knew nothing about the Biblical account of Lucifer's reign here on Earth (Ezekiel 28:12-18; Isaiah 14:13-14). That it took place before Adam and before Lucifer's rebellion, which ended with the first flood account in the Bible (Jeremiah 4:23-28). Schmidt apparently only knew text knowledge of the Bible and had no inspired knowledge of Biblical text given by God. He knew and taught other pastors about Biblical studies without knowing how to do it properly with God's inspiration himself. Therefore they knew and memorized the text without understanding how to search for the complete information on each topic. Therefore he and those he taught didn't know how to put the puzzles of the Biblical mysteries together to receive the full understanding.

Therefore Schmidtih suggested these stories were the source of the Biblical accounts as Abraham and Sarah who both grew up in Ur, which was in Sumeria and probably knew all the Sumerian stories by heart. However since Schmidtih never knew about the Lucifer flood I believe Schmidt surmised, because of the similarities in these stories that the Sumerian stories spoke of Noah's cataclysm. Therefore he was totally unaware of Lucifer's reign, rebellion and that Lucifer's story ended in a flood cataclysm many thousands of years before Adam.

Also, the Sumerian version of the Tower talks of 50 technicians who employ mysterious technology to dispatch 300 observers to the space stations in the stars. Therefore the Sumerian tower had a different more technically advanced purpose than the Biblical Tower of Babel. It seems it was a space gate of some sort offering observers access to the space stations. So to the non-modern 1890's mindset of Schmidt this was totally unbelievable to even consider it had happened. He didn't even have a clue as to what the ancient text was speaking about. To us today we recognize what was being described here. We still can't do it but we believe we will eventually develop the technology necessary to do this.

However back in the late 1800s Schmidt could only comprehend the tower and not its purpose. He therefore connected it to the Tower of Babel. To Schmidtih in the late 1800's the Sumerian tower's described purpose didn't make sense so he mistakenly thought they were speaking of the Biblical Tower and that was a costly mistake. We have to understand that back then all Christians were taught that the Earth had only come into existence with Adam. They had no knowledge, Biblical or otherwise, that the world had existed and was populated before Adam. Their concept of the technology like flying machines, advanced construction methods and equipment Lucifer and his angels brought with them was totally non-existent. So in Schmidt's mind since nothing existed before Adam this Sumerian Tower had to be the Tower of Babel. The ultimate proof for him might have been that the Sumerian story ends in a cataclysmic flood. Again we must consider that he had never even heard of Lucifer's civilization nor that a flood from God destroyed it as we have learned about in Chapter 2 (Ezekiel 28; Isaiah 14; Jeremiah 4).

Schmidt made the mistake of not doing an in-depth study of the Bible himself before coming to his conclusion. Therefore when Schmidt read the Sumerian text and noticed the similarity in the stories he suggested the Hebrew and Christians copied stories from them. He was tried for Heresy and fired from his tenured position. Today we have the advantage of having access to the many in-depth studies that have been done on the Bible. We are aware, or should be, of the translation errors that have occurred. Some of which I have pointed out in Chapter 2. Unfortunately very few people take any time to study the Bible for themselves and that has led to many false teachings. If archeologists and scientists would keep the Bible as their base truth and interpret their findings from there I'm quite sure our understanding of the truths revealed would be very different today.

Let's continue. It turns out that the Sumerians weren't the only race that kept a Kings List. The Egyptians also kept a record of kings. This information is found from two separate sources. The first source of this other list was from the Papyrus of Turin, which was found by Bernardino Drovetti in 1820. He was an Italian traveler who found this Papyrus in Luxor (Thebes), Egypt. It was transferred to the Egyptian Museum in 1824 and is recorded as Papyrus Number 1874. The second and confirming source for this Egyptian Kings List is the Palermo Stone which is kept in Palermo Italy. It was found by a visiting French archeologist in 1895 and was translated and published in 1902 by Heinrich Schafer. If you add up the length of time for each king the Egypt's Kings List covers a period of 36,000 years. Logic would dictate that Lucifer came to Earth and began in one area (probably Sumeria) then expanded this project to other areas of the Earth. Hence the time difference. But that would make complete sense. Now these rulers of Egypt on these lists were said to be the Nechuru and that these kings were gods themselves. That they came down from the sky. This ties in completely with the Biblical account that these were some of Lucifer's angels.

Please note that we have answered the questions of:

1. Who are the visitors from the skies? They were angels created by God

2. Where did they come from? They came from God's dimension and Universe

3. Did these visitors have advanced technology? Yes.

4. Was knowledge shared with the population of the Earth? Yes

5. Did these visitors help the people of Earth engineer and construct huge mega-structures around the world? Archeological evidence tells us yes they did.

6. Do they travel in flying machines? Yes, God's technology was and is light years ahead of ours. Today

we call them UFOs or the new Air force designation of UAPs).

7. Is there a plausible timeline for when this might have occurred? Yes.

8. Are there good and bad entities among these visitors? Yes. We are dealing with fallen angels and angels that are with God's kingdom

9. We've seen that if we understand scripture properly and then discern history, archeological, geographical and scientific discoveries through the Biblical lens, then we find the confusing mysteries of our past and present begin to make sense. Through the Biblical lens, we have a firm foundation of knowledge that helps us to understand the mysteries of civilizations past, present and future. Without it, we are just stumbling around in the dark.

CHAPTER 10

How to Use this Information

The information you have learned in this book should have shown you that you have to view information that comes to your attention through the lens of the Bible. You must also apply your common sense and logic when coming to a conclusion. Let's see how that process helps us to deal with this Facebook post. So using the scriptures along with common sense and logic we can figure out what happened with Adam and Eve.

Even the picture they have used is misleading in the context they are presenting. Adam and Eve did have three children after the fall and they were all boys. However the three boys never lived together. Scripture tells us that after the fall and expulsion from the Garden they had Cain and Able. I'll make the assumption that they lived for about 20 years before having their argument over the sacrifices and Cain killed Able

with a rock. After this death Cain struck out on his own. Eve conceived again and had her son Seth. Now Adam was 130 years old when Seth was born (Genesis 5:3). So all three boys never lived together and this picture is wrong. This post is trying to also imply that since they only had three boys there was no way for them to father generations of children down to us. I've also seen a similar post asking where they got their wives from. Basically saying scripture is lying to us because without wives children would be impossible. I would bet whoever posted these has never read a Bible and was reacting to information someone else had given him or her. Common sense tells me that since Seth was conceived after Abel's murder and was born when Adam was 130 years old there is a time period of 130 years to be accounted for. So let's work backward from Seth's birth because that's the first mention of age in Adam's timeline in the genealogies.

I'll assume there was a mourning period after Abel's death before Adam and Eve knew each other again. So let's say they waited 3 months and Seth was born 9 months later when Adam was 130 years old. We've already guessed that Cain and Abel were around 20 years old when the killing took place. Then math tells us Adam was around 129 when the murder took place. That would mean Adam was roughly 109 years old when God tossed them out of the Garden. My speculation could be off several years, but this would roughly be accurate. Logically that would mean Adam and Eve would have lived in the Garden for 100 plus years before they fell.

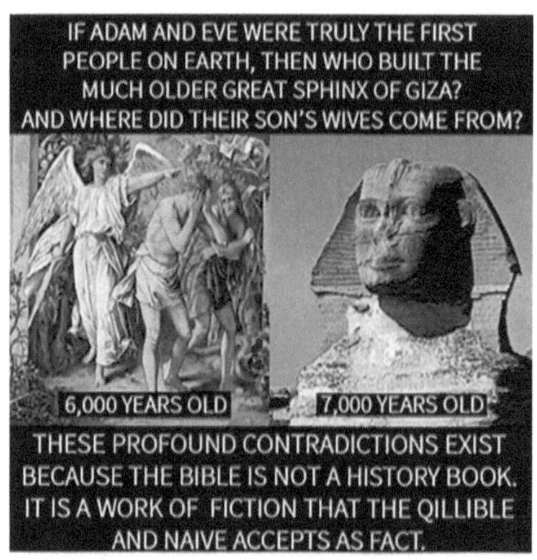

Remember that God told them in Genesis 1:28 to go forth and replenish the Earth. So being a vibrant and healthy couple they would have had child after child and when those children reached puberty they would have had children and so on for over 100 years. Adam and Eve weren't created and then fell to temptation within the first week as some unlearned people would have us believe. That means that Adam and Eve weren't the only ones thrown out of the Garden of Eden. No! All their children and children's children that were born before the fall came out with them. This pool of people is where Cain's and Seth's wives came from. These are the people that wanted to kill Cain so God put the mark on Cain to protect him from being killed by them.

Genesis 4:15 And the Lord said unto him, Therefore whosoever slayeth Cain, vengeance shall be taken on him sevenfold. And the Lord set a mark upon Cain, lest any finding him should kill him.

These are also the people that helped Cain build the first city of Enoch, named after his first son.

> Genesis 4:17 And Cain knew his wife; and she conceived, and bare Enoch: and he builded a city, and called the name of the city, after the name of his son, Enoch.

Come on people, all you have to do is actually read the Bible to find this information before making silly posts and calling the Bible untrue. It's not hard just try it. There is an interesting parallel here, because of Adam's sin all of his children were accounted as sinners as well. This flows down to us even today. We see therefore by applying the same principle to Jesus 'the righteous one paid for our sins on the cross.' All who believe in Him, His righteous life, His death paying for our sins, and His resurrection have our sin debts paid in full.

> Colossians 2:13-15 **13** And you, being dead in your sins and the uncircumcision of your flesh, hath he quickened together with him, having forgiven you all trespasses; **14** Blotting out the handwriting of ordinances that was against us, which was contrary to us, and took it out of the way, nailing it to his cross; **15** And having spoiled principalities and powers, he made a show of them openly, triumphing over them in it.

And His righteousness is applied to us through faith.

> Ephesians 2:8 For by grace are ye saved through faith; and that not of yourselves: it is the gift of God: **9** Not of works, lest any man should boast.

> Romans 5:8 But God commendeth his love toward us, in that, while we were yet sinners, Christ died for us. 9 Much more then, being now justified by his blood, we shall be saved from wrath through him. 10 For if, when we were enemies, we were reconciled to God by the death of his Son, much more, being reconciled, we shall be saved by his life. 11 And not only so, but we also joy in God through our Lord Jesus Christ, by whom we have now received the atonement.

12 Wherefore, as by one man sin entered into the world, and death by sin; and so death passed upon all men, for that all have sinned: 13 (For until the law sin was in the world: but sin is not imputed when there is no law. 14 Nevertheless death reigned from Adam to Moses, even over them that had not sinned after the similitude of Adam's transgression, who is the figure of him that was to come. 15 But not as the offence, so also is the free gift. For if through the offence of one many be dead, much more the grace of God, and the gift by grace, which is by one man, Jesus Christ, hath abounded unto many. 16 And not as it was by one that sinned, so is the gift: for the judgment was by one to condemnation, but the free gift is of many offences unto justification. 17 For if by one man's offence death reigned by one; much more they which receive abundance of grace and of the gift of righteousness shall reign in life by one, Jesus Christ.)

Here we also see how the world is confused about what we preach in the church. We teach that everything started with Adam only 6000 years ago. But, the children are taught in schools that the world began millions or perhaps billions of years ago. They offer up evidence from archeology, paleontology and science to back up their claim. The church offers the Genesis creation story and firmly hold to 6000 years and no more. Unfortunately, the church has ignored the story in Ezekiel, Isaiah and Jeremiah, which tells of Lucifer's rule here on Earth. I went into great detail in chapter 2 regarding this and even compared the two catastrophic floods the Bible talks about in chapter 3. The Devil, who is not stupid by the way, recognized the opening the church handed to him on a silver platter. By firmly holding to the impossible timeline of 6000 years the church allowed the Devil to offer the theories of Evolution and The Big Bang. He caused subtle mistranslation at specific points in scripture to hide the fact he and his angels were ever here. We also discussed this in detail in chapter 2.

2 Corinthians 3:14 But the people's minds were hardened, and to this day whenever the old covenant is being

read, the same veil covers their minds so they cannot
understand the truth. And this veil can be removed only
by believing in Christ.

The Devil is intelligent, has powers and has been plying his skills of lies and temptation for thousands of years. So let's not hide that fact. He has inspired people to create Museums which proudly display dinosaur fossils so Schools can take young children on day trips to see this evidence. The schools teach our children that it takes 10,000 years to create a fossil. They are then taught in church that nothing existed before 6000 years ago and this confuses them. Which teaching do you think causes a bigger impression on young minds? Now if the church would only learn and understand what the Bible teaches about Lucifer's rule here on Earth and the fact that there were two floods we could credibly tell them the Biblical story. Then the schools and teachers would have to be defending their position.

Bible believing parents would have credible information to explain to their children that this process of creation has gone on for a long time and Adam was the beginning of this last phase. The children or parents could explain that the Bible tells us that when Lucifer ruled here on Earth as Covering Cherub (Ezekiel 28:14) he ruled over hominids (an earlier version of man that was different from Adam Jeremiah 4:22, 24). Lucifer and his angels built magnificent cities and nations worldwide. We could help the children and anyone else who was interested understand that Archeologists have found and are finding today the ruins of these cities. As I explained in chapter 5 it is impossible to date rocks and therefore the age estimates they place upon these ruins are totally wrong. These ancient ruins date back thousands of years before Adam and as you've seen in chapter 5 we couldn't even build them today. We can't even move the huge stones at Baalbek let alone harvest them. Yet the ancients did, but the stones used for construction back then certainly weren't cut with stone hammers and chisels.

Now how does this information here in help us answer the question of dinosaurs and correct the misinformation our children have been taught in school? I've shown you in chapter 2 that the Bible does teach about Lucifer's rule here on Earth, his rebellion and the eventual destruction of all he had created during that time. We know he was already a fallen angel when he tempted Eve in the Garden so logic tells us that all of that activity occurred before Adam. Actually many thousands of years before Adam as I've shown you in chapters 2, 3 and 9. Let's keep the timeline general and not too specific. So God had to have created dinosaurs long ago before Adam and that would mean they were around when Lucifer ruled Earth. Archeologist and paleontologists all claim they were around for hundreds of millions of years. As you've seen in those same chapters those scientists have been proven wrong more times than I can lists here with their time estimates. Plus they've been caught faking, hiding and destroying evidence while trying to prove their pet theories.

So use the information in this book and their science to prove them wrong. Let's at least start correcting the lies they've been feeding our children. Remember in chapter 3 I pointed out that Museums were not displaying the fossilized skeletons of modern day birds, which were found mixed in with the dinosaur bones in the South African Bone Bed. They found 90 different species of modern birds and not one is displayed in any museum around the world. Why? **Because that is evidence of no Evolution and when evidence found does not fit with the accepted dogma it is hidden from the public**. Now the next information got out to the public before they could stop it, but shortly after it has been hidden and no one is talking about it. I assure you if this had happened in the 50's, 60's or 70's it would have been headline news. Walter Cronkite would have been all over it. Yes I'm that old.

In 1993 at Hell Creek, Montana, Dr. Mary Schweitzer discovered dinosaur blood cells. Had you heard of this? I hadn't until Creation Magazine published an article about it. All other media ignored this story. Why? **Because it does not fit with the accepted dogma so it is hidden from the public**. See the pattern? All of a sudden finding viable blood cells in a Duckbilled dinosaur that was supposed to have died out 65 million years ago is not news or interesting to anyone in the media? Well, it certainly didn't fit into the accepted dogma they are teaching our children. See chapter 3 for more info on what else they found at Hell Creek. Even the teachers probably don't know about this and that would really make for a stimulating conversation. Don't you think? Now if someone asked the question, 'Since it takes 10,000 years to form a fossil and the South African Bone Bed is totally fossilized, but the Hell Creek Montana Bone Bed is not fossilized. Would that mean these animals died in separate flood events?' And, 'Would the fact that the Hell Creek dinosaurs, since they aren't fossilized didn't die 65 million years ago but died in Noah's flood 4300 years ago?'

I would bet that the teacher would be sweating by this point, at least frustrated and wishing they had called in sick this day. I want you to understand I'm not against teachers and I understand they were taught the same false information as they are teaching. However it is time to stand up to the false dogma they are teaching. We need to research for ourselves and not just accept what is presented as the absolute truth. All the information in this book is readily available in the Bible, books, you can find those in Libraries kids, on the web and a lot on YouTube. Stimulate your minds and do your own research. It takes time and effort but you'll find it well worth it.

We know for a fact the Intellectual Elites in the world are pushing the Theory of Evolution. If the revelations from Hell Creek doesn't push their efforts backward then the general population is definitely not awake. Let's put another nail in their proverbial coffin. Since Darwin's publication in 1859 there have been many frauds put forward as proof of this missing link. **1)** Java man in the 1890s **2)** Ramapithecus Man in 1904 **3)** Piltdown Man in 1912 **4)** Nebraska Man in 1920 **5)** Lucie in the 1930s. All have been proven to be frauds. However these frauds are still seen in full color renderings in school textbooks and displayed in museums around the world as facts that men evolved from apes. There have also been numerous fakes put forward for the missing links of evolution in the animal kingdom. All eventually proved to be fake, but no retractions have ever been given.

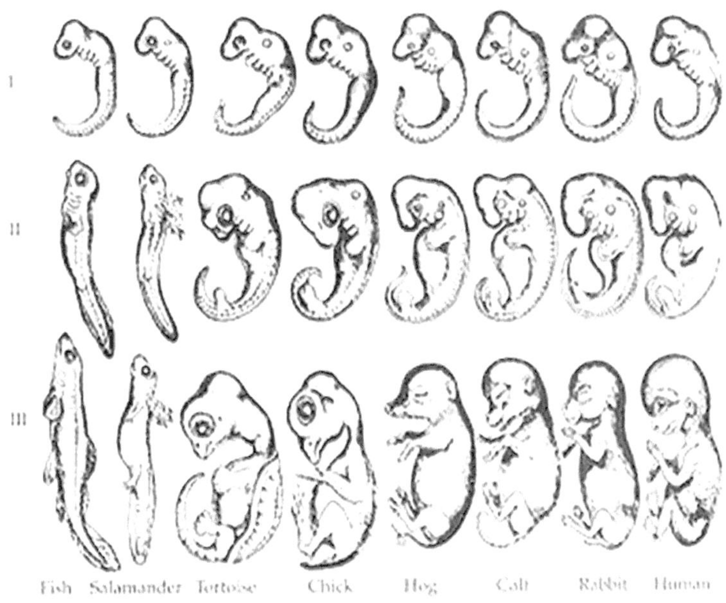

German biologist Ernst Haeckel included illustrations of the embryological stages of vertebrates in a series of books published between 1868 and 1908. Fudging the data, he placed the drawings into a comparative grid, highlighting similarities between species and blurring differences. The results are highly inaccurate.

Haeckel wanted to convince his readers that all vertebrates share a common ancestor, and that, as he put it, "ontogeny recapitulates phylogeny" – our embryonic development repeats our evolutionary past. This aphorism was soon disproved, but the use of Haeckel's drawings persisted, particularly in education. There were waves of criticism, from the 1870s when the drawings were published, up to 1997 as Haeckel's "fraud" was rediscovered and exploited by creationists.

In this sumptuous book, Nick Hopwood, a science historian, examines how and why Haeckel made his drawings, and the use made of them since. His clever detective work takes him into the Haeckel archives in the German town of Jena, discovering the original drawings and even the woodblocks. At the other end of the story, he explores how Haeckel's drawings appeared in postwar textbooks in the UK and the US. These images have been copied and reinterpreted from the late 19th century on, and insights from writers shed a fascinating light. For example, Scott F. Gilbert, author of a 1985 developmental biology textbook, inadvertently used Haeckel's images. There seems to be no length of fraud these people haven't tried and are trying to perpetrate on a seemingly uninterested world. The church really has to stand up for the truth.

Since the Devil doesn't mind inspiring fraud, after all he is the father of lies (John 8:44), I don't feel bad about putting forward a speculation. I was wondering if there was any evidence geologically of a worldwide extinction. I wondered about this because of Jeremiah 4:23-28, which describes the total (extinction level) destruction of the world by God after Lucifer's rebellion was defeated. We covered that in detail in chapter 2 of this book. I thought there might be evidence of that event and it turns out there just might be. There was an event called The Younger Dryas which according to geologists occurred roughly 14,500 years ago. The evidence for this is found in the strata of our Earth and that being a black line of strata which is found all over the world. Scientists say that this black strata indicates that an extinction event occurred worldwide. Nothing survived.

Scientists are not in agreement as to what caused The Younger Dryas, but whatever it was it occurred worldwide. Evidenced by the black line of strata. They are also confident that this event brought on a mini Ice Age, not a normal one but one like a flash freeze occurring instantly. This may be the cause of what is baffling scientists in the north.

They are perplexed by the frozen giants (Mammoths) of northern Siberia and Alaska. This is well documented in Joseph C. Dillow's book The Waters Above in chapter 10. The discovery of these totally frozen giants with flesh so well preserved it was edible when they were found. Ivory tusks so well preserved that they looked like they had just came from Africa. It is documented that these frozen carcasses have been found here since 1712 if not before. These giants are from the Pleistocene Age which scientists say ranged from 2.6 million years to 11,700 years ago. What baffles the scientists the most is that whatever happened back then occurred so quickly that some of these giants were frozen standing up. Autopsies revealed that the buttercups and grass in their stomachs was undigested and there was even grass and buttercups in their mouths that hadn't been swallowed before they were frozen. An adult mammoth is estimated to have weighed up to 8.2 metric tons (9 tons) so how cold did it have to suddenly get to freeze that whole animal before it could swallow? Yet it happened. It is well documented with hard forensic evidence.

Other well preserved specimens such as this Siberian rhinoceros have also been found in this area of the world. In the Dating Game section of chapter 3 I have shown you some of the problems and errors that have occurred when our experts try to date things from our past or estimate time periods for how long a species of animals lived on Earth. Because of those documented errors I believe the Pleistocene Age ended with the Younger Dryas Event roughly 14,500 years ago. Since no one knows for sure what caused that total extinction event I will put forward my speculation that the destruction described in Jeremiah 4:23-28 occurred roughly 14,500 years ago.

It's a description of worldwide destruction of cities, nations and all life on Earth at that time because God was so angry at what Lucifer had done. Then to complete the destruction of life God turned all the lights of the universe off (Jeremiah 4:28) and that would have caused a total deep freeze. Only God could have done this so quickly that the mammoths didn't have time to swallow. Surely Christians today have very little understanding of the true power of God. I believe The Younger Dryas Event was the end of Lucifer's civilization here on Earth. This would account for all the unexplainable ruins that are being found all over the Earth and under the seas today. It also explains why none of the construction techniques used back then are understood today even with our current technology levels. The Forgotten Civilization of Lucifer existed for close to 270,000 years (according to the Sumerian Kings List) before it was destroyed in a cataclysmic flood event. This is my speculation, but it seems to line up with the Bible, geological, archaeological, scientific and historical evidence that is currently available in 2023.

The Big Bang Theory confuses me just a bit. You see that theory seems to start out okay saying the Universe started as just a single point and I agree. That point being Father God speaking the substance of faith into this dimension. Jesus (then called the Word) took that substance and from that formed the galaxies, stars, planets (Hebrews 11:1-3; John 1:1-3). Now I don't understand that totally, but I can get my mind around it being possible. The Big Bang folks say it started with a big explosion which apparently caused a lot of dust and over billions of years these little pieces of dust started sticking together randomly and eventually formed planets. My problem continues in that the Astronomers tell us Earth is in a solar system within The Milky Way galaxy.

The Astronomers tell us there are 200 billion galaxies in our Universe and the total number of planets in the Universe is incalculable. However they estimate there are around 100 billion planets in the Milky Way galaxy. Wow? I don't know about your mind but mine goes 'holy cow, that's a lot of dust accumulation. What the heck was the size of the object that exploded at the beginning? I mean it must have been enormous to be able to form 200 billion galaxies from just the dust of that one explosion.' Do you see the problem here with their theory? You see the substance of faith is never ending. As long as God the Father has faith the substance that faith creates is never ending in supply. So creation keeps going and the Astronomers themselves tell us the Universe is still today expanding, because God is still believing.

Their Big Bang theory has more problems. The next problem for the Astronomers to explain is the process of Retrograde. There is a regular orbital resetting process among the planets. It happens to each planet once a year and some planets experience it more frequently. **Retrograde** looks like the planet is moving on its course as it normally does. Then it slows down and eventually stops. After this it appears to move backward on its orbital course for a bit. Next it looks like it is slowing down and stopping again. After this it will reverse into its normal speed and direction. To me this smacks of Intelligent Design. This is not an accidental process as it occurs on a regular bases to every planet in our solar system. There is no way the planets accidentally experience this on a regular basis. I've explained it in more detail in chapter 6. So when you are confronted with The Big Bang Theory ask them to explain why the planets go into Retrograde. (Sourced from Story in the Stars by Joe Amaral)

The next problem for the Astronomers to explain is the Constellations. They have been in place around the Earth for thousands of years. We know this because they have been recorded and documented as such by civilizations down through the millennia. I've shown you in chapter 6 that there are pyramids around the world that are exactly aligned to Orion's Belt. The ancients called Orion's belt the Light of Heaven. So when Jesus said He was the Light of the World He was tying Himself back to the Orion

The last Neanderthal giant

Constellation's story. The ancients knew it depicted a hunter with club and shield. This constellation and the many others have not moved out of place since their creation by God. They tell the story of the Messiah and how He's fighting the dragon, the devil. These were not created by accidental collision. They were intelligently designed to tell the Messiah's story not meant to forecast futures as some believe the horoscopes do.

The next lie that we can address is that even though the Bible tells us there were giants walking the Earth there has been a concerted effort to hide or destroy any evidence which would prove that to be true. Xaviant Haze's book 'Ancient Giants of the Americas' documents very well both the giants' existence and the cover up. Also I have laid out additional information that I could find with pictures where they were available in chapter 8. However even I found that this information is quickly disappearing. Haze documents that the private company called The Smithsonian Institute has played a very large part in this cover up and I agree. Here are some additional photos that have come across my path recently.

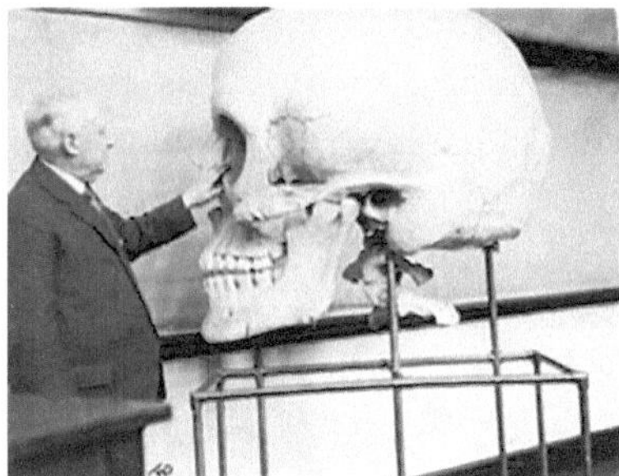
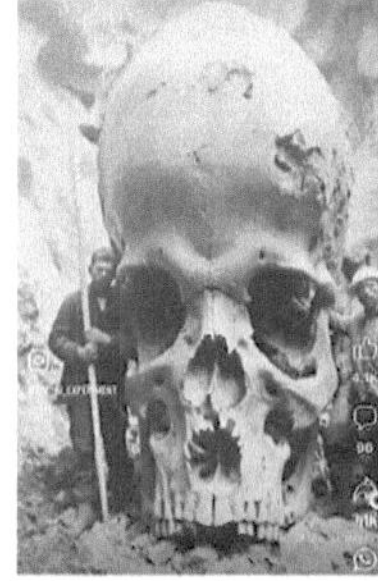

Portal de Boca Norte del Túnel de Las Raíces

I feel that what I presented in Chapter 8 and these new photos show enough proof for you to doubt what the Intellectual Elites of the world are telling us and that being that giants only existed in myths and legends. The church has to wake up and start defending the Bible, but I guess we have to start believing its truths first.

In ancient India I have shown you that they were worshiping fallen angels. The temple carvings of their gods present images of multiple armed and in some cases multiple faced beings. Those stone images reflect the Bible's descriptions of Cherubim and Seraphim angels. India has many other types of gods represented not only in their temples but also in their ancient stories, which I went over with you in chapter 9. We must remember that God loves variety and color in His creations. We just have to look at nature to see that reflected in our own time. So a huge variety of angelic types and colors does not surprise me in the least. India's ancient stories speak of the wars these angels fought against each other. And the Bible refers to Lucifer ruling the nations with anger.

> Isaiah 14:6 He who smote the people in wrath with a continual stroke, he that ruled the nations in anger…

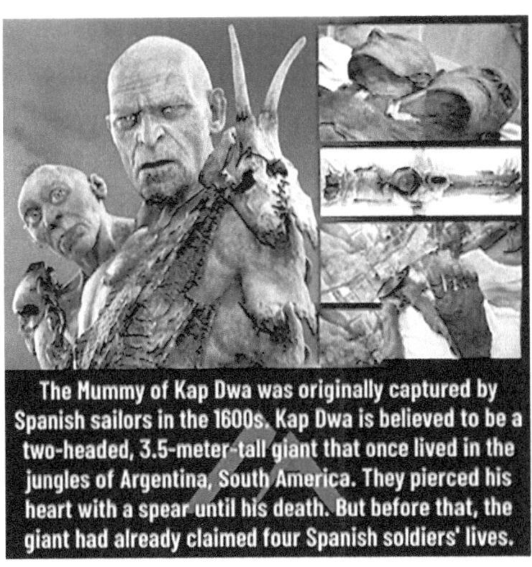

Lucifer was anything but a benevolent ruler. We discussed much more in chapter 9. The fallen angels not only taught the hominid men of that time how to make weapons but also how to conduct war against perceived enemies. I'm sure these angels trained their armies and then pointed them in the direction they wanted them to go. But they also taught them amazing techniques in construction.

Without a doubt these are beautiful and artful at the same time we have to admit they would be impossible to hand carve as the world's Intellectual Elites would have us believe. The precision and mathematical accuracy in the architecture and interiors is impossible without advanced knowledge and technology.

Alright here's another impossible piece of construction that the Intellectual Elites of the world want us to believe it was accomplished with hammer and chisel. Impossible! How did the carver drill a 0.5 MM hole, perfectly straight, through the head of this statue? This statue is made out of granite and this hole is 400 MM long. It would be difficult today, but thousands of years ago?

I hope the information I have provided you in this book will help you in your witnessing efforts. At the very least this information will start a dialogue and you'll be able to answer some of their questions.

BIBLIOGRAPHY

The Dake's Annotated Reference Bible, King James Version text, by Fibis Jennings Dake. Copyright in 1961 and published by Dake Bible Sales Inc. P.O. Box 1050, Lawrenceville, Georgia 30246

Charles Capps teaching on *The World That Was*, rebroadcasted on YouTube June 7, 2021

Chariots of the Gods, by Erich von Daniken, copyright 1999, published by Berkley

The Late Great Planet Earth, by Hal Lindsey, 1970, published by Zondervan

The Gospel in the Stars, by Joseph A. Seiss, illustrated version, copyright 1972, Kregel Publications, Grand Rapids, Michigan

Story in the Stars, by Joe Amaral, copyright 2018, publisher Faith Words, New York and Nashville. A very good book which gave me insights into Retrograde and NASA' ability to track historic astrological events.

Ancient Giants of the Americas, by Xaviant Haze, copyright 2017, The Career Press, Inc. 12 Parish Dr. Wayne, NJ 07470

The Waters Above, by Joseph C. Dillow, copyright 1981 by The Moody Bible Institute of Chicago, Chapter 10 The Riddle of the Frozen Giants

The Book of Enoch, Translated by R.H. Charles, copyright 2018, digireads. com Publishing

Mahabharata, by Maharishi Vyasa, manufactured by amazon.ca Bolton, Ontario

The Ramayana, by Ramesh Menon, copyright 2001, published by North Point Press, New York

The Complete Apocrypha, 2018 edition, published by Covenant Press

Pictures were acquired through various hardcopy and online resources

Other information was gathered from programs on Netflix, YouTube, and Ancient Aliens